SHELLEY

AND

SYNESTHESIA

SHELLEY AND SYNESTHESIA

GLENN O'MALLEY

te sociam studeo

LUCRETIUS, I, 24

NORTHWESTERN UNIVERSITY PRESS

1964

Open access edition funded by the National Endowment for the Humanities/Andrew W. Mellon Foundation Humanities Open Book Program.

Glenn O'Malley. Shelley and Synesthesia.
Evanston, Ill.: Northwestern University Press, 1964.

ISBN 978-0-8101-3862-9 (paper)
ISBN 978-0-8101-3863-6 (ebook)

Printed in the United States of America

Original edition LCCN 64-19452

FOR

My Mother and Mildred

ACKNOWLEDGMENTS

MY FIRST DEBT in writing this book is to Professor Carlos Baker, who guided me through completion of a doctoral dissertation on the same subject for Princeton University. He knew best how much help I needed, and he was ever ready to help.

At various stages in my work, Professor Wallace W. Douglas was most kind in offering invaluable advice and criticism. Others whose friendship and encouragement have meant more to me than they can imagine are Professors Walter H. Evert, Hugh B. Staples, and Donald T. Torchiana.

Parts of this book reproduce or reflect three earlier efforts. Chapter 1 uses material from "Literary Synesthesia," which appeared in the *Journal of Aesthetics and Art Criticism*, 15 (1957), 391–411. Chapter 2 incorporates "Shelley's 'Air-Prism': The Synesthetic Scheme of *Alastor*," *Modern Philology*, 55 (1958), 178–187. Some of Chapter 5 was summarized in a talk, "*Adonais:* Myth and Mythology," given at a meeting of the Midwest Modern Language Association, Lincoln, Nebraska, Spring, 1962.

I wish to thank Dean Moody E. Prior for helping to make funds available both for the typing of the manuscript and for publication. Finally, I am grateful for the assistance and understanding of Mrs. Joy Neuman of the Northwestern University Press.

February, 1964

CONTENTS

SHELLEY

AND

SYNESTHESIA

1

INTRODUCTION: POETICAL HARLEQUIN

I

THIS STUDY of Shelley's poetry has grown out of investigation into his striking use of intersense analogy, now best known as synesthetic imagery and conveniently definable as language which describes one sense experience in terms that "belong" to one or more of the other senses. Such transfers among sense vocabularies (e.g., "strident color") are still sometimes regarded as eccentric or even abnormal in origin,[1] so that a writer's frequent or otherwise extraordinary use of them may invite special notice along psychological lines. I want to stress at the outset that my concern is primarily literary—that is, to concentrate on Shelley's imaginative adaptations of this sort of language and of notions related to it. But this is about equivalent to saying that synesthetic expression in Shelley most interests me as a means, not as an end in itself, for perhaps its most important aspects are symbolic and structural. Certainly one would be ill-advised to consider it apart from contexts. Shelley characteristically associates synesthetic imagery with certain of his favorite subjects or themes, with symbolic patterns, and even with the ordonnance of entire poems. In short, he makes synesthesia subserve elaborate, subtle aesthetic designs. And by following what he does in this way, I hope to reveal hitherto untold meaning and craft in much of his most important work.

What others have done to similar ends is far from negligible and will properly be noticed in a moment. First it is necessary to remark that while others have clearly demonstrated the importance of Shelley's synesthetic usage and pointed directions for further investigation, their findings have been either slighted or, if known and valued, left undeveloped. Particularly in the last ten years or so, in which one ambitious and pretty much comprehensive Shelley study after another has appeared, I find generally little and often no awareness that the most "Shelleyan" of his poems require sharp attention to synesthetic aspects of his art. Rogers, Wilson, and Bloom—to mention only three most recent authors of big books on Shelley—write almost as though his synesthesia could be dismissed entirely.[2] As more than four decades have passed since Erika von Siebold (later Mrs. von Erhardt-Siebold) published her indispensable study of Shelley's synesthesia,[3] and more than one decade since Richard H. Fogle had to redirect notice to this side of the poetry,[4] what is one to think? Probably such neglect prevails partly because literary synesthesia itself is even now misprized or ill comprehended and partly because Shelley's craftsmanship on the whole is still badly undervalued, so that on either score or both people have been unable or disinclined to perceive how skilled, various, and intricate his synesthetic practice is. Hence what has so far been well said of this practice may seem close to the last word.

Acquaintance with the work of Mrs. von Erhardt-Siebold and of Fogle might suffice to launch this introduction. But it may help generally to review along with theirs kindred studies by June E. Downey and Oscar W. Firkins.[5] The four taken together have contributed in the last half-century just about all that has seemed worth knowing of Shelley's synesthesia. And since the history of their contributions is itself decidedly and suggestively not one of steadily developing knowledge and since, too, their influence on general treatments of Shelley's poetry has been slight, it will be instructive as well as convenient to proceed chronologically. Their studies range from 1912 to 1949 and reflect to some extent the uncertain advance and uneven quality which during that time characterized much of the research and criticism in the whole field of literary synesthesia.

In 1912 June Downey's article "Literary Synesthesia," which included her remarks on Shelley, was still pioneer work among English-language explorations of the subject.[6] To be properly appreciated, it should be set against a background well represented by Irving Babbitt's *The New Laokoon.*[7] Perturbed by synesthesia in nineteenth-century French literature, Babbitt believed that the use of intersense analogies was at best aesthetically trivial and at worst symptomatic of psychological and spiritual disorder. "For the critic of art and literature," he wrote, "they [*audition colorée* and 'similar phenomena'] are interesting and curious, but scarcely anything more. They concern more immediately the student of psychology and medicine, and in some cases the nerve-specialist." [8] Miss Downey's approach to the subject, though mainly a psychologist's, rejected this simple, arbitrary diagnosis. To begin with, she wished to distinguish carefully between "true" and literary (or "pseudo") synesthesiae.[9] By true synesthesia she meant experience, not necessarily pathological, which leads a person to speak as though he has actually *heard* light or color (*audition colorée*), or *seen* sounds (tonal vision). Literary synesthesia, as investigations into imagery of Keats, Poe, Swinburne, and others convinced her, did not necessarily reflect confusions at the sensory level (and in all likelihood rarely reflected any) but was primarily imaginative exploitation of assumptions that data of one sense could somehow resemble those of another. This suggests that Miss Downey may somehow have been less critical of synesthetic language offered in evidence by psychologists' subjects than of poetic metaphor. But for intelligent study of intersense analogies in literature her distinction between "spontaneous" (true) and "deliberate" (literary) comparisons marked a great advance from Babbitt's naïveté.

In examining Shelley's intersense analogies, Miss Downey conducted psychological tests with eleven verse fragments "the phrasing of which was synesthetic," and also "recorded every case of sense analogy in 4,000 lines from the poetry." [10] She was not concerned with statistical tabulation of the analogies or with their relationship to contexts. She confined herself simply to determining, with help from certain "readers' " responsive musings, whether any of Shelley's analogies expressed true synesthetic experience. Her results agreed with what she found true of other poets—namely, that Shelley's "departure from the facts of true synaesthesia . . . suggests an imaginative use of sense analogies rather than a genuine duality of sensory impressions." [11] Departing from the "facts" meant that the poet favored analogies which were seldom or never reported by psychologists' informants, such as analogies involving odors with sights and sounds. Shelley's boldness with odor similes—

> music so delicate, soft, and intense,
> It was felt like an odour within the sense—[12]

seemed especially convincing evidence that his synesthesia was only imaginative.[13] But she was struck generally by lack of "spontaneity" in his comparisons, by his artful deliberateness.

Mrs. von Erhardt-Siebold's invaluable but much overlooked comments on Shelley's synesthesia appeared in a long, two-part monograph, published just after World War I. The most comprehensive and detailed of principally literary studies of synesthesia, it dealt nominally with English poetry of the nineteenth century. The first part, however, treated matters connected with most aspects of the whole subject: definition, historical origin, eras and areas of cultivation, aesthetic value, and so on. The second, a series of chapters on Keats, Tennyson, Poe, Rossetti, Swinburne, Francis Thompson, and others, is especially notable for attempting to do justice to ways in which each poet adapted intersense analogies to his own style. The longest chapter she devoted to Shelley, claiming his use of synesthesia to be the most significant in all English literature.[14]

Though agreeing with this claim, I would point out at once that her judgment of Shelley's pre-eminence and certain features in her description and evaluation of his synesthetic practice are tainted by one serious limitation. She wrongly believed, in common with Babbitt and others, that literary synesthesia was almost exclusively a Romantic stylistic innovation, exploited successively by the Germans, English, and French. The error persisted because scholars were overly impressed with the stimulus given to synesthetic usage and speculation by the once-famous Father Castel's invention of a color organ, in the early part of the eighteenth century.[15] This sharply restricted perspectives on the history of synesthesia, a study which has since been extended to antiquity,[16] and led her to judgments which now must be rejected or modified. For example, a sense of Shelley's eminence or oddity in synesthetic experiment must be altered by taking into account similar experiments in English poetry of the seventeenth century; and I am sure that his practice would be better understood if related to Dante's.

According to Mrs. von Erhardt-Siebold, Shelley was the first English poet to employ synesthesia consistently. It may be surprising to learn, therefore, that she found only some fifty synesthetic images in twenty thousand lines.[17] (Here I confess not knowing how to count images.) But she rightly argued that this computation had little meaning by itself, especially if one observed how the images function in context. She noticed that Shelley tends to group them in climactic passages which attempt to describe existence in millennial or quasi-mystical states, as in the fourth act of *Prometheus Unbound,* or in *Epipsychidion* when the subject is union with Emily. In such passages intersense analogies not only suggest a surpassing variety, refinement, and complexity of sensuous experience, but also, by evoking a "harmony" or synthesis of all sensations, emblem a kind of supersensuous unity. This synthesis, incidentally, which she called *Sinnesuniversalismus* (and may be likened to Baudelaire's "métamorphose mystique/ De tous mes sens fondus en un"),[18] she held to be the ultimate goal of all Romantic experiments with synesthesia, and Shelley among English poets approached it most nearly. Within the climactic passages, moreover, synesthetic segments themselves climax Shelley's descriptions of sense experience: first come crowded references to data of various senses considered separately, this itself suggesting the influence of *Sinnesuniversalismus;* then the suggestion is confirmed when the description culminates in synesthetic fusions.[19]

In *Epipsychidion,* for example, Shelley heaps up questions about what Emily's beauty may be likened to (lines 56ff.), goes on to descriptive statements which, though more sensuous than the questions, only verge on synesthetic comparisons (lines 75ff.), and then brings all to an extreme pitch (lines 91–111):

> The glory of her being . . .
> Stains the dead, blank, cold air with a warm shade
> Of unentangled intermixture, made
> By Love, of light and motion: one intense
> Diffusion, one serene Omnipresence,
> Whose flowing outlines mingle in their flowing,
> Around her cheeks and utmost fingers glowing. . . .
> Warm fragrance seems to fall from her light dress
> And her loose hair; and where some heavy tress
> The air of her own speed has disentwined,
> The sweetness seems to satiate the faint wind;
> And in the soul a wild odour is felt,
> Beyond the sense, like fiery dews that melt
> Into the bosom of a frozen bud.

All this has the following important implications. Shelley's synesthetic expressions, though frequent enough throughout his career and discoverable in various parts of his verse, do not characteristically appear in isolation or as incidental decoration. Usually they cluster in contexts which handle somewhat philosophical subjects having to do with relationships between sense and spirit, and between variety and unity. Hence they should be expected most often in works in which these themes are prevalent, his so-called "ideal" or "visionary" poems. Within such poems, a passage containing intersense analogies should be understood to form only the most salient portion of a general scheme of imagery, the whole of which may in a sense be considered synesthetic. Finally, as the foregoing indicates, his use of synesthesia is broadly symbolic in the best meaning of the word—"harmony" of the senses being at once sign and part of a greater harmony.

With so much to thank her for, I believe it only fair to emphasize Mrs. von Erhardt-Siebold's opinion that Shelley's intensive experiments with synesthesia failed aesthetically. Holding to a rule that synesthesia succeeded only as a moderate heightener of poetic suggestiveness, she judged that Shelley's practice was self-defeatingly excessive, especially in its elaboration of sustained synesthetic patterns. Given the aims of his "ideal" verse, Shelley should have modulated synesthetic language so as to preserve body and weight in sensuous intimations of a supersensuous One, not—as it happened—to etherealize them. She concluded that Shelley's notoriously pronounced intellectuality led him to overreaching ingenuity and costly disregard for concreteness.[20]

O. W. Firkins' *Power and Elusiveness in Shelley*, published in 1938, contained a chapter dealing with synesthesia under the title "Assimilation." Like Mrs. von Erhardt-Siebold, Firkins saw Shelley's intersense analogies as an extreme form of a general tendency in his poetry.

Shelley, he said, cultivated abstract expression of "ideas which combine momentousness of import with indistinctness of material." [21] And, pursuing this, Shelley not only preferred to describe impalpable properties such as light, wind, sound, and odor, but also, going a stage further, liked to catalogue, or in a manner coordinate, even these in their simplest, least-differentiated forms: "sound, and odour, and beam" (*The Sensitive Plant,* I, 92), "motion, odour, beam, and tone" (*Epipsychidion,* line 453). Beyond such coordination (so-called because the elements manifest the operation of one all-pervasive Force), came the still further stage of synesthetic comparison or fusion. As Firkins put it, "The mere conjunction or collocation of light, sound, odor, and their correlates is not enough for Shelley; he must unite them still more closely by means of comparison, or even by a kind of fusion, identification, or transformation of one into the other." [22]

Firkins' way of putting these and other remarks alerts one to the fact that this accomplished scholar had read little or nothing about synesthesia. And he admitted in effect that intersense analogies in literature as a rule escaped his notice: "Shelley's proneness to this form of simile is extraordinary, if not unexampled; I remember no other author in whom it occurs with like frequency. Dante's phrase *dove il sol tace* applied to sunset is startling enough to be itself almost a demonstration of the rarity of this species of comparison." [23] What this says of Shelley may pass, but that queer demonstration of "rarity" indicates, besides a misreading of Dante, surprising obliviousness to synesthetic expression in other writers. I call attention to this shortcoming with no wish to belittle Firkins, whose book, despite posthumous publication, is mostly admirable. It illustrates how strangely elusive intersense analogies can be, even to those who seem well prepared to recognize them: Firkins responded keenly to Shelley's, but elsewhere noted them rarely; others have valued them in the Metaphysicals or French Symbolists, but missed them somehow in the English Romantics. And the shortcoming actually stresses the value of Firkins' "Assimilation" chapter as completely independent testimony to the importance of its subject. Highly perceptive testimony it was, for in commenting on some thirty passages of Shelley's poetry Firkins showed remarkable insight into their display of conscious artistry, including "wit."[24] He was especially suggestive, again resembling Mrs. von Erhardt-Siebold, when he observed in agreement with his general views on Shelley's aims that sometimes the synesthetic "interfusions" seemed so intense as to demand metaphysical explanation.[25]

R. H. Fogle, last of the four authors under review, included a chapter on synesthesia in his excellent comparative study of Shelley's and Keats's imagery. His approach was consciously independent of Mrs. von Erhardt-Siebold's and had the peculiarity of "stretching . . . privileges of definition" in order to treat as synesthetic, not only "imagery which purposes chiefly to establish relationships between the different modes of sensation," but also any "instantaneous fusion of the concrete and abstract."[26] Stretched so, his definition was much too broad, and he in fact, small wonder, seldom invoked those privileges. But his conception of synesthesia remained somewhat hazy. This was extenuated perhaps by Fogle's dominant concern to vindicate Shelley's sensibility against modern detraction. He was arguing, for example, that New Critics should recognize and appreciate "tension" and "paradox" in Shelley's straining to resolve the concrete variety of things into abstract unity. So, discussing Shelley's synesthetic imagery, he said it revealed contradictory fidelities to the One and the Many. True to the One, Shelley synesthetically transposed those properties of things that seemed most amenable to synthesis: he at once avoided "unusual straining of the bounds of normal perception" and strove to effect easy, almost imperceptible passage of one sensation into another.[27] But, against this, Shelley retained sharp awareness of strictly individual qualities of phenomena, his intersense analogies evincing "exquisite feeling for subtle gradations of coloring, changes of sensuous tone, degrees of relationship in sensation." [28]

Nevertheless, Fogle conceded more than once that Shelley's synesthetic expressions tended to reflect thought as opposed to sensation. Thus, compared with Keats's, they are "likely to culminate in abstraction," are "symbolic, not naturalistic," are "less complex, less sensuous, and less spontaneous." [29] This emphasis, carefully qualified, recurred in his well-phrased summary, which substantially agreed with Mrs. von Erhardt-Siebold: "Synaesthesia in Shelley is the poetical expression of a conscious, intellectual quest after a cosmic and psychic unity, in which the merging into Oneness of disparate physical phenomena symbolizes the ideal unity toward which the spirit strives. In the final stage of this process sense and spirit are themselves one, fused by intellect, sensation and emotion into an imaginative whole." [30]

Fogle had little to say about relationships between Shelley's synesthesia and contexts or specific symbols. Though he understood that the primary function of Shelley's synesthetic imagery was "to aid in carrying out the purposes of the poem in which it occurs," [31] the plan of his book precluded giving this much attention. He did write of a concentration of synesthetic images in *Prometheus Unbound*, Act IV, and in *To a Skylark*. In the latter, he felt, Shelley employed intersense analogies more consistently than anywhere else, and he spent several brilliant pages analyzing how the lark's song is compared to various forms of light and flowing water and, "by some obscure process of association," to these combined:[32]

> From rainbow clouds there flow not
> Drops so bright to see
> As from thy presence showers a rain of melody. (33–35)

These four writers, besides testifying amply to the importance of synesthetic expression in Shelley's poetry, have provided materials for a remarkably uniform description of its character and function. To summarize details of such a description here would be unnecessarily tedious. I would only emphasize the points which offer the most valuable suggestions for further investigation. These are (1) that Shelley's intersense analogies are broadly adapted to the purposes of poems in which they occur; (2) that in such poems they therefore stand in a developmental relationship to other but related kinds of imagery, being climactic expressions of sensuous harmony; and (3) that they have symbolic relevance to philosophic themes of unity and harmony, which recur from poem to poem. The most useful hint along these lines springs from Mrs. von Erhardt-Siebold's observation that synesthetic motifs dominate contexts in which Shelley describes millennial or quasi-mystical states of being. These suggestions suffice to insure at the least a highly favorable estimate of Shelley's achievement in one area of modern literary experiment.[33] At best they strongly support the view, common among Shelley scholars but notoriously unacceptable to many influential critics, that the imagery of his "ideal" poems, far from being a hypnotic haze of sense impressions, is a complex vehicle of great imaginative significance. Students of synesthesia may even feel that what has been described of Shelley's achievement approaches the symbolic and architectonic limits of this stylistic resource. But I hope to show that all this is only a beginning.

II

Neither Shelley himself, in essays and letters, nor contemporary commentators on his publications help us to ascertain much about his knowledge and opinion of synesthesia. His reviewers, to be sure, reacted sharply to many of his intersense analogies, especially in such later works as *Prometheus Unbound, Epipsychidion,* and *Adonais.*[34] Their comments are uniformly unfavorable, and their method of listing synesthetic images with other "absurdities" shows that these critics were either unable or unwilling to distinguish such images as a special kind. For instance, the following remarks on *Epipsychidion* characterize the general tendency to confound intersense analogies with other examples of Shelley's stylistic "anarchy" (the passage referred to is evidently that quoted on page 9): ". . . what a number of adjectives, and how strangely coupled with nouns! Only hear—'Odours deep, odours warm, warm fragrance, wild odour, arrowy odour. . . .' [This is poetry whose] odours may be felt, and its sounds may be penetrated—its frosts have the melting quality of fire, and its fire may be melted by frost. . . . It is a poetical phantasmagoria. . . . Things may exchange their nature, they may all have a new nature, or have no nature." [35] In similar vein, his reviewers highlighted synesthetic expressions to prove that Shelley's verse was full of nonsense, indulged in conceits, invited parody, and generally was either thoughtless or perverse. All such criticism rather surprisingly yields no evidence that the writers had ever encountered intersense analogies in any poetry other than Shelley's, or had any notion that their use might be artistically justifiable. Ridicule and ignorance prevailed; even witty reference in *Adonais* to Echo as a "shadow of all sounds" provoked only the derisive label "Nonsense—physical." [36]

In a singular case, a critic in *The Quarterly Review* showed exceptional insight into one of Shelley's synesthetic conceits, but still denounced it as absurd. He observed that a "characteristic trait of Mr. Shelley's poetry is, that in his descriptions he never describes the thing directly, but transfers it to [*sic*; to it?] the properties of something which he conceives to resemble it by language which is to be taken partly in a metaphorical meaning, and partly in no meaning at all." [37] To analyze this trait, the reviewer cited from *The Sensitive Plant* a stanza in which, as he said, Shelley describes the hyacinth in "quaint and affected" terms:

> the hyacinth purple, and white, and blue,
> Which flung from its bells a sweet peal anew
> Of music so delicate, soft, and intense,
> It was felt like an odour within the sense. (I, 25–28)

"It is worthwhile," he wrote, "to observe the train of thought in this stanza. The bells of the flower occur to the poet's mind; but ought not bells to ring a peal? Accordingly, by a metamorphosis of the odour, the bells of the hyacinth are supposed to do so: the fragrance of the flower is first converted into a peal of music, and then the peal of music is in the last line transformed back into an odour. These are the tricks of a mere poetical harlequin. . . ." [38] Lumpish enough, this surpasses in literary alertness what Miss Downey, as we have seen, later made of the same music-odor comparison.

How much and in what ways Shelley resented or relished such criticisms, we can only guess. All his prose, indeed, offers but one fairly plain allusion to synesthesia and its possible implications for literature and thought. This appears in *A Defence of Poetry* (written in 1821): "Their [poets'] language is vitally metaphorical; that is, it marks the before unapprehended relations of things and perpetuates their apprehension. . . . These similitudes or relations are finely said by Lord Bacon to be 'the same footsteps of nature impressed upon the various subjects of the world'—and he considers the faculty which perceives them as the storehouse of axioms common to all knowledge." [39] Shelley, as a note of his indicates, here refers to a passage in Bacon's *De Augmentis Scientiarum*, Lib. III, Cap. i, in which one of the "axioms common to all knowledge" reads: "Fidium sonus tremulus eandem affert auribus voluptatem, quam lumen, aquae aut gemmae insiliens, oculis. . . ." (The cognate passage in *The Advancement of Learning*, Book Second, Section V, 3, reads: "Is not the delight of the quavering upon a stop in music the same with the playing of light upon the water?") From this it may be inferred that for Shelley synesthetic analogies, like Bacon's comparison of a musical tremolo to shimmering light, assist in that metaphorical unveiling of "the permanent analogy of things" which he mentions elsewhere in the *Defence* and associates in a Pythagorean strain with the poet's "echo of the eternal music." [40] And some such drift of thought, with all its inclination toward a metaphysic of universal correspondences, would no doubt have been a main current in any Shelleyan defense of literary synesthesia.

The seeming ignorance of Shelley's reviewers is cause for wonder. Modern researches give the impression that, the eighteenth century having rung from beginning to end with synesthetic speculation, most writers and critics of the Romantic era were schooled to a sophisticated appreciation of intersense analogies. By 1813, for example, allusions to once-famous synesthetic marvels associated with Locke, Newton, and Father Castel must have risked being jejune as proffered in Madame de Staël's *De l'Allemagne* (published in London). She wrote: "Analogies among various elements of the physical world serve to confirm the supreme law of creation, variety in unity, and unity in variety. What is more astonishing, for example, than the correspondence between sounds and forms, between sounds and colors? . . . Sanderson, blind from birth, said that he imagined the color scarlet to be like the sound of the trumpet, and a savant has wanted to make a harpsichord for the eyes, which through the harmony of colors might parallel the pleasure that music produces. We continually compare painting to music, and music to painting, because our feelings reveal analogies where cool observation would mark only dissimilarities." [41] The "astonishing correspondence" between sounds and colors had been fixed with mathematical precision in Newton's *Opticks* (1704), where it was recorded fondly, if not obsessively, that measurements of spaces occupied by the seven spectral colors yielded proportions like those which obtain among the octave intervals.[42] This discovery, conceivably because it lent color to Pythagoras' harmony of the spheres, was a rich source of enchantment and befuddlement throughout the eighteenth century, though Albert Wellek, the most reliable and comprehensive historian of synesthesia, no doubt went too far in asserting that it affected almost every branch of intellectual culture.[43]

Mme. de Staël's "Sanderson" (i.e. Nicholas Saunderson, an English mathematician, 1682–1739) harks back erroneously to a celebrated, anonymous anecdote in Locke's *Essay concerning Human Understanding* (1690): "A studious blind man, who had mightily beat his head about visible objects, and made use of the explication of his books and friends, to understand those names of light and colours which often came in his way, bragged one day, That he now understood what *scarlet* signified. Upon which, his friend demanding what scarlet was? The blind man answered, It was like the sound of a trumpet." [44] By this Locke meant to demonstrate the absurdity of merely verbal attempts to understand "simple ideas," and for some time one illustrious writer after another (Steele, Fielding, Johnson)[45] delighted in exposing the blind man to ridicule. Yet as early as 1735, according to Albert Wellek, Father Castel found the scarlet-trumpet analogy only "natural";[46] toward the end of the century, Erasmus Darwin, with revolutionary semantic insight, suggested that it might not be "quite so absurd, as was imagined";[47] and, as we have seen, Mme. de Staël obviously believed that there had been more than one way of taking the anecdote. (Already about 1712 Shaftesbury was recalling in a sympathetic but somewhat bungled context "the story of the deaf man's likening scarlet to a trumpet"; this was not published until 1914, however.)[48]

The savant who proposed to construct an ocular harpsichord was, of course, the Jesuit Castel.[49] Partly influenced by Newton, whose color theory he eventually rejected in favor of one of his own, Castel at first attended primarily to physical parallels between sound and light, but then went on and on speculating about their subjective counterparts. In 1725 he announced in the *Mercure de France* that he would display the validity and viability of light-sound analogies by means of an ocular harpsichord, or color organ, through which one could "translate" musical compositions.[50] Unfortunately, promise and performance proved to be two different things. Skeptics, along with mechanical and aesthetic obstructions, forced the inventor to refine his theories, especially those regarding sense perception. At last, despite marked resourcefulness, Castel himself conceded that beyond a certain point *le son est le son et la couleur est la couleur.*[51] All along, nevertheless, he stubbornly defended his basic concept that objective and subjective parallels tallied and even committed himself to a program of demonstrating the comprehensiveness of such parallels through additional harpsichords for taste and smell. By such fanciful elaborations and the great celebrity of his color organ, this *Don Quichotte des mathématiques,* as Voltaire called him,[52] made conjecture about systematic, detailed synesthesiae an eighteenth-century commonplace.

For over twenty years before the publication of *De l'Allemagne*, acquaintance with all this lay open to English readers in the writings of Erasmus Darwin, whose pages on synesthesia, though few enough, gave the most substantial contemporary survey of the subject in our language. He treated it twice: first in a prose "Interlude" in his poem *The Loves of the Plants* (first published, 1789; frequently reprinted in *The Botanic Garden*), and again in a similar addition to *The Temple of Nature* (1803).[53] In the "Interlude," a comment on the "sisterhood" of various arts,

Darwin brought synesthetic speculation to bear mainly on relationships between the "sister-ladies, Painting and Music," though clearly having uppermost in mind not painting but some temporal chromatic muse. He reviewed Newton's computations for the spectrum-gamut parallel, suggestively calling it "metaphysical" as well as mathematical, and then described how, following this parallel, one might "produce a luminous music": "This might be performed by a strong light, made by means of Mr. Argand's lamps, passing through coloured glasses, and falling on a defined part of a wall, with moveable blinds before them, which might communicate with the keys of a harpsichord, and thus produce at the same time visible and audible music in unison with each other." [54] He noted, however, that Father Castel was said to have tried the idea "without much success." [55]

A fresh effort to perfect the color organ might be facilitated, thought Darwin, if advantage were taken of new scientific evidence for the "curious coincidence between sounds and colours." His own son, Dr. Robert Darwin, investigating ocular spectra, or complementary afterimages, demonstrated "that we see certain colours, not only with greater ease and distinctness, but with relief and pleasure, after having for some time contemplated other certain colours"; but since "the pleasure we receive from the sensation of melodious notes . . . must arise from our hearing some proportions of sounds after others more easily, distinctly, or agreeably; and as there is a coincidence between the proportions of the primary colours and the primary sounds," Robert concluded "that the same laws must govern the sensations of both." [56] Thus scientific father and scientific son joined in confounding physical and psychophysiological "evidence."

Erasmus Darwin added to the confusion by asserting abruptly that all this supported the sisterhood of music and *painting,* not "luminous music," but then drew the redemptive inference that these arts could justly "borrow metaphors from each other; musicians to speak of the brilliancy of sounds, and the light and shade of a concerto; and painters of the harmony of colours, and the tone of a picture." [57] And, consequently, a blind man might not absurdly guess from such metaphors that scarlet was very like a trumpet sound.[58]

While Shelley's reviewers may have known nothing of this in Mme. de Staël and her predecessors, his own acquaintance with such synesthetic speculation probably began in school days at Syon House Academy (1802–1804) and Eton (1804–1810). One of the most exciting and important influences on his youth, long recognized as such, was Adam Walker, who delivered scientific lectures at both schools.[59] A respectable amateur encyclopedist of science, but also somewhat bizarrely imaginative, Walker liked to inspire his listeners with brave conjectures and sweeping syntheses. Not surprisingly, therefore, one discovers that his lecture on optics, as published in *A System of Familiar Philosophy* (1802), carefully rehearsed the findings by which Newton showed that the spectrum intervals "answer to the intervals of the diatonic scale." [60] This "wonderful conformity" between the two inclined Walker to believe that "our scale in the major key had its foundations in nature." [61] Discussing red, Walker did not fail to recall blind man and trumpet.[62] Strangely, he did fail to treat "luminous music," but, still in the same lecture, revealed himself perhaps ready to welcome every kind of synesthetic organ by explaining how "All our senses may be said to be modifications of the sense of feeling." [63] Observations of this kind Shelley may have heard more than once and read as well in Walker's book.[64]

If thus made, Shelley's acquaintance with synesthesia would have been powerfully reinforced by his later reading in Erasmus Darwin. Unfortunately, this reading and its effects are hard to pin down. As early as July, 1811, Shelley wrote T. J. Hogg that he was amusing himself by reading Darwin, and on December 17 and 24, 1812, he included *Zoönomia* and *The Temple of Nature* in orders to booksellers.[65] Shelley scholars generally assume a strong Darwinian influence on *Queen Mab* (begun, probably, about April, 1812; finished sometime in 1813) and take for granted that, though Shelley never mentions it, *The Botanic Garden* was a prime element in that influence.[66] Very likely, therefore, Shelley knew both of Darwin's surveys of synesthesia, the "Interlude" on the arts in *The Botanic Garden,* and the note in *The Temple of Nature,* interestingly entitled "Melody of Colours."

These conjectures about Shelley's youthful knowledge are worth making for what they suggest about the beginning and development of his synesthetic art. Consider first the bent of eighteenth-century concern with intersense analogies, which is typified in Darwin, except for his insight into the significance of synesthetic transfers in fairly ordinary speech. All this synesthetic speculation was involved in a suggestive jumble of physical, psychological, and aesthetic observations and notions; it concentrated on the two most "intellectual" of the senses, sight and hearing; it tended to fix on the marvelous, like precise links between tones and colors; and it favored the rationalistically systematic, like "luminous music." Behind most of it there must have been some faith like that of Castel, who believed that the ultimate unity of all phenomena could be glimpsed through universal correspondences. Now Shelley's synesthetic usage reflects much of this, sometimes rather crudely, sometimes in very subtle refinements. He, too, inclines toward the intellectual and, especially in early works, concentrates on sight and hearing; even his later, quite considerable experiments with the "lower" senses are somewhat abstract. He is given to exploiting the wonderful, though with markedly progressive artistic responsibility; the spectrum-gamut parallel I believe he had in mind from the start and took as a sort of model for more complex "marvels." His synesthetic patterns smack definitely of the systematic, wit-worked, and conceited. And, as his allusion to Bacon hints, he often uses intersense analogies as though they partook of an ultimate unity or harmony.

III

However his knowledge of synesthesia originated and grew, there is no point in Shelley's career at which his verse does not reveal some use of it. In the juvenilia, his drafts on it appear to be casual and slight. Most instances can be written off as nothing more than faded metaphors or synesthetic transfers of ordinary speech. In *The Retrospect: Cwm Elan, 1812,* for example, *radiance* is *imbibed,* just as everyone "drinks in" this or that; again, there is reference to weaving a "web of talk," a metaphor found in the *Iliad.*[67] The commonplace "eloquence" of eyes is toyed with awkwardly in a fragment ascribed to 1810.[68] Isolated, these have little or no interest for us. But a remarkable feature of his career is its general consistency, even from so early a period as that of the juvenilia. Few aspects of his mature verse lack anticipations in the writings which run through

Queen Mab (privately printed, 1813). Hence one might trace a connection from the insipid "feeding" image of *The Retrospect,* through a series of similar images in *The Revolt of Islam* (composed, 1817),[69] to complex transformations of such imagery in the synesthetic scheme of *Adonais* (1821). Corresponding developments of the "web of talk" and of ocular eloquence might also be followed. It is more important to note, however, how the feeble images of *The Retrospect* hint that Shelley is already experimenting with synesthesia to articulate an "ideal" theme.

A meditative landscape poem of about 150 lines, *The Retrospect* notably foreshadows *Alastor, Epipsychidion,* and other works in which intense personal emotion is expressed in visionary terms. The important lines for my point occur in a passage which contrasts a scene once beheld in "coldest solitude" with the same scene revisited

when peaceful love
Flings rapture's colour o'er the grove,
When mountain, meadow, wood and stream
With unalloying glory gleam,
And to the spirit's ear and eye
Are unison and harmony. (3–8)

What requires explanation here is the total suppression of auditory imagery in lines which insist on "unison and harmony" in the spirit's response to light and color. Shelley writes as though he intended the reading *ear-and-eye* (line 7) to account for the implied correspondence between visible and audible. One might object that instead of synesthetic intent we should see here a typically Shelleyan looseness of phrasing. But the reading I conjecture for this passage of *The Retrospect* is precisely the sort required by

Shelley's practice in kindred later poems. Simple and weak enough, it is a highly suggestive anticipation of his synesthetic development.

Though this development already takes an interesting turn in *Queen Mab,* written about the same time as *The Retrospect,* it matures only in those "ideal" poems, starting with *Alastor,* which are securely advanced beyond the juvenilia. Shelley naturally excluded synesthetic expression from works like *The Cenci* and the unfinished *Charles the First,* which were intended for the stage and in any case were partly undertaken in deference to his wife Mary's objections to "visionary rhyme." [70] But not all of his more or less esoteric poems employ synesthetic schemes. *The Witch of Atlas* and the lyrical drama *Hellas,* for example, disclose none that I can see. Conversely, *The Revolt of Islam,* which Shelley hoped would reach a fairly wide audience, includes synesthetic expressions and notions as part of an elaborate symbolism. Hence among Shelley's longer works (and I shall deal mainly with them, not the lyrics) there has been no easy or automatic prescription for this study. Still, certain of the "visionary rhymes" are clearly distinguishable for their synesthetic significance. In chronological order of composition, these poems are *Alastor* (1815), *Prometheus Unbound* (1818–1819), *Epipsychidion* (1821), *Adonais* (1821), and *The Triumph of Life* (1822). In these five works, intersense metaphor and symbolism form essential parts of the total structure. And in them, together with *Queen Mab, The Revolt of Islam,* and some short pieces, it is possible to trace a somewhat steady elaboration of synesthetic schemes. Here again, however, no rule of thumb applies. *Prometheus Unbound,* for example, presents what is probably Shelley's most ambitious, most intricate experiment, and I therefore keep its exposition till last. With exceptions of this kind allowed for, a brief preliminary survey of my procedure in tracing the evolution of these schemes may be useful.

Chapter Two focuses on *Alastor* to demonstrate how Shelley, probably influenced by the spectrum-gamut equation, parallels Aeolian or natural music with rainbow light, and closely associates synesthetic perception of that parallel with the nature and destiny of the narrative's nameless hero. Aeolian music and the rainbow are basic symbols, which I take to be interchangeable signs of a unity pervading all phenomena, this symbolic duality itself implying synesthesia. Perhaps the most interesting feature of the poem is Shelley's way of showing, through the hero's visionary sensibility, that music can be perceived as color and vice versa. Throughout, the hero is symbolized as a kind of Aeolian harp; but his delicate responses are at times best explicable in terms of prismatic refractions of a divine light. In fact, Shelley's conception of the hero (for which he may have drawn on an obscure eighteenth-century speculation) makes him an "air-prism," a symbolic, synesthetic fusion of prism and Aeolian harp. Considering this symbolism in *Alastor*, I think it worth stressing that synesthetic imagery taken alone scarcely begins to reveal how much the notion of intersense analogy contributes to the total structure of the poem. Also, it should be noted that, after *Alastor*, Aeolian music and the rainbow repeatedly appear, often together but on occasion separately, when Shelley introduces synesthetic visionary motifs; that is, they may function more or less as synesthetic signs or signals.

Chapters Three to Six all deal in large part with synesthetic aspects of a system of imagery and symbolism which I shall call the Venus complex. Its focus is the morning and evening star, which Yeats in an essay of 1900 proclaimed as the most important of all Shelley's symbols.[71] Chapter Three, "Melody of Light," treats the Venus complex and its synesthetic aspects with special reference to *The Revolt of Islam, The Triumph of Life,* and *To a Skylark.* To understand the synesthesia of the Venus complex, one must realize that Shelley accepted the Pythagorean notion of the music of the spheres and accommodating parts of the Ptolemaic astronomy for imaginative purposes, and then refined upon them. For Shelley, indeed, harmony of the spheres is probably the most powerful member in a symbolic family which includes Aeolian music. The mystic, potentially all-pervasive harmony of Pythagoras was traditionally, of course, an influence which emanated from revolutions of the crystalline heavenly spheres. Shelley adopted this notion, but equated the influence with that of a "revolution" of love, and so justified localization of supernal harmony in the third Ptolemaic sphere of Venus and in the light of her planet. Synesthetically, therefore, he fuses the harmonies and illuminations of love in the light of Venus, or in the music of her sphere. This explains, for instance, how he can refer in *The Triumph of Life* to the "sphere whose light is melody to lovers." (The passage containing the phrase, incidentally, has great importance for interpreting *The Triumph of Life* and for discussing relationships between Shelley's synesthesia and Dante's.)

The Venus complex first appears in *The Revolt of Islam,* where Shelley endows it with a rich variety of symbolic meanings, personal, social, and metaphysical. Its synesthesia bears on both the narrative structure and the conception of the leading characters. In fact, intersense metaphor helps specially to bring out certain allegorical and symbolic relationships in the poem which hitherto have been grasped weakly, if at all. But the synesthetic Venusian scheme of *The Revolt* is most valuable as an aid in understanding its variations in later works. *The Revolt,* longest of Shelley's poems, is generally impressive for trying out on a large scale many of the themes, symbolic structures, and even figures which Shelley cultivated intensively in his great Italian period. This seems to be sadly ignored in some recent Shelley studies. It is certain, at any rate, that *The Revolt* offers invaluable schooling for detecting synesthetic subtleties which appear in later work.

Here, partly in connection with *To a Skylark,* may be noticed a problem that confronted Shelley in refining synesthetic details of the Venus complex. One drawback was that a certain symbolic or intellectual emphasis made it synesthetically lopsided; that is, while the light of Venus was naturally perceptible in her planet, the music of her sphere, of course, remained entirely imaginary. In one way this perfectly suited Shelley's purposes, because synesthetic perception of harmony in starlight corresponded to the ability of rare spirits like Pythagoras to hear spheral music. All the same, Shelley apparently was dissatisfied that the scheme allowed no direct appeal to any sense other than sight. One plausible solution was to reify supernal harmony by exploiting a broad Pythagorean relationship between the spheral and an Aeolian (or natural) music. Not content with this, Shelley strove to make more specific additions to the Venus complex. Some he found in the song of skylarks and nightingales, which, possibly taking a hint from Milton, he associated generally with spheral music and specially with aspects of the planet. Having done this, Shelley quite characteristically went on to treat the bird song as synesthetic also. In *To a Skylark,* for example, when the unseen lark is likened to a star unseen in daytime, its song is compared to the light of Venus. This is addition or compensation with a synesthetic vengeance. Flowers served too. To bring them into the Venus complex, Shelley depended on age-old conceits which interchange heavenly flowers and earthly stars, as well as on aspects of plant physiology which suggest light-odor comparisons. In *Adonais* he went further, taking advantage of classical myth, combined with a pun on the Greek word *aster*, to strengthen bonds between flowers and the morning and evening star (Adonais being an aster, both flower and star). As with bird song, Shelley's procedure with flowers is clear: he incorporates a natural source of odor into the complex and then makes it bear light.

These additions to the Venus complex illustrate how Shelley sought to balance symbolic and naturalistic elements in his synesthetic constructions. His ultimate goal in such efforts was to create an acceptable embodiment, or source, of total synesthesia—that is, an agency which might appeal to all of the senses individually *and* to the faculty which perceives correspondences among them. And these efforts, which are discussed in Chapter Four, reached their greatest intensity in *Epipsychidion.*

The synesthetic scheme of *Epipsychidion* can be sketched out rather simply if it is seen as an extension of the one in *Alastor,* since it also depends on adaptations of prismatic refraction. In *Alastor,* whatever the implications of the harp-prism fusion for all the senses, not just sight and hearing, it suffices to imagine that light can be "refracted" as music and, conversely, that an ideal, Aeolian harmony can be "refracted" as colors. In *Epipsychidion,* imagery and symbolism bring out the implications of the air-prism scheme and require us to comprehend how a supernal "illumination" can be broken down into "colors" that affect all the senses, and affect them so that synesthetic analogies disclose an underlying unity. Shelley's main problem in achieving this was, of course, to discover an adequate "prism." There are at least two such prisms in the poem, both incarnations of supernal light. One is the goddesslike Emily, whom a fragment associated with *Epipsychidion* refers to as "an embodied Ray/ Of the great Brightness." The other is the enchanted island to which Shelley imagines himself and Emily escaping—an island within which an "atom of th' Eternal" burns "like a buried lamp." As "embodied rays," both Emily and the island emit "beams" which affect all of the senses synesthetically. Both, too, are interrelated parts of the Venus complex, which dominates the symbolism and the synesthetic expression of the whole poem. Grasping all this should greatly enhance our appreciation of unity in *Epipsychidion.*

Chapter Five deals exclusively with *Adonais,* where synesthesia is again an aspect of the Venus complex. Exposition is much aided here by what distinguished scholars like Hungerford and Baker have already done to explain how the elegy adapts the Venus-Adonis myth along with symbolism of the morning and evening star.[72] To be sure, more recent writers on *Adonais,* especially Wasserman, have tried to diminish Venus's role.[73] Close attention to synesthetic complements, however, should help to reestablish the dominance of the Venus complex, and reveal that Hungerford and Baker have been the best guides to understanding the highly intricate, but comparatively "public," art of this poem. For its synesthetic aspects, we need not puzzle about rather esoteric devices like air-prisms and embodied rays. We know that Shelley, though frankly proud of his artistic achievement in handling the traditional pastoral elegy afresh, eagerly hoped that it should be well and widely read for the sake of Keats's memory.[74] Probably, therefore, he tried to make its synesthetic patterns more accessible than those of poems like *Alastor* and *Epipsychidion*. He deserved to succeed in this, I believe. At any rate, it seems to me that the synesthesia of *Adonais*, particularly its interweaving of references to stars (light and fire), flowers (odor), and music (or echoes), should yield to relatively easy, if somewhat lengthy, exposition.

The sixth and last chapter before the conclusion concentrates on *Prometheus Unbound*, which by virtue of its aim, scope, and complexity must be judged Shelley's greatest imaginative effort, and in which, as already mentioned, the synesthetic scheme is proportionately ambitious. In the later *Epipsychidion*, *Adonais*, and *The Triumph of Life*, synesthetic aspects of the Venus complex are closely conjoined with the focal symbol, the morning and evening star. In *Prometheus Unbound*, where the triumph of love brings world harmony, both human and natural, the Venus complex is appropriately prominent, but Shelley articulates its synesthetic devices with such figurative comprehensiveness and intricacy that their relationship to his star symbolism may often seem obscure. This can be appreciated more readily if we recognize that the predominant metaphorical pattern of the poem is concerned with the natural cycle of water in all its forms—cloud, mist, dew, rain, stream, sea, and so on. Since the goddess Venus was born of the sea, one connection between the metaphorical pattern and Shelley's primary symbolism becomes clear. Again, certain metaphors, as well as some machinery of the drama, may recall the light and harmony of the third sphere. Nevertheless, the poet's concern with water figures and symbols is so predominant that it is they which require principal attention in the synesthetic scheme. Hence it will be appropriate to label this scheme the "stream-of-sound," a term which Woodberry applied long ago to what he called the drama's "cardinal image." [75] The stream-of-sound, swelling progressively, is Shelley's symbolic means for establishing world harmony. So important is this synesthetic scheme in his total structure that it affects almost every aspect of the drama, including personifications and scenic arrangements. By the fourth and final act, its development is such that the entire ordonnance of the concluding scenes depends upon it. Understandably, therefore, the synesthesia of the *Prometheus* presents expository difficulties of considerable magnitude. These, fortunately, can be somewhat lessened by turning to a compact and comparatively explicit use of the stream-of-sound in *Orpheus,* a dramatic fragment which I believe to be Shelley's, though his authorship has been much questioned.

Since in this survey so much has been said of symbolism, especially of harmony and illumination, it may be in order to add a final introductory word about the naturalistic side of Shelley's intersense analogies, and about his use of the so-called "lower" senses in relation to the "higher" or "more intellectual" ones of sight and hearing. As with questions about the extent to which Shelley's literary practice may reflect personal proclivities toward synesthetic perception, so any consideration of his success in balancing the abstract and naturalistic in synesthetic expression will probably be influenced a good deal by what one already thinks of his general characteristics as a poet. I think his synesthetic practice does incline toward the abstract and toward heavy emphasis on light and sound. But such a judgment must be carefully qualified. First, as already suggested, there is much evidence that Shelley tried to compensate for abstract tendencies in synesthetic constructions, and to include within them data of the lower senses. This indicates to me a highly responsible, as well as ambitious, artistic effort to realize all that was implied in his idea of total synesthesia. How far he got can be measured to a fair extent by comparing *Alastor* with *Epipsychidion* or *Adonais*. And then if, even in such later poems, the balance seems to dip on the intellectual side, it should be remembered as no little extenuation that Shelley's symbolic adaptation of synesthesia was in itself an extremely brilliant achievement. In variety and refinement it exceeds, in my opinion, every similar achievement ascribable to other poets, even Dante and Baudelaire.

2

ALASTOR: THE AIR-PRISM

I

SHELLEY's first important use of synesthesia appears in *Alastor, or the Spirit of Solitude,* a narrative in 720 lines of blank verse, written late in 1815 and published the next year. The use is schematic and depends mainly on Shelley's way of disposing and combining two sets of images and symbols throughout the poem. One set comprises references to rainbows and prisms; the other to Aeolian or "natural" music and to Aeolian instruments. These two image-symbol sets or motifs are repeatedly juxtaposed not only in *Alastor,* but in poems written at every stage of Shelley's career. The recurrent juxtaposition, which has apparently never been noticed, may seem glaringly obvious once it is pointed out. But the synesthetic combination of the two is another matter. To recognize it we must understand how it was possible for Shelley to treat prisms and Aeolian harps as interchangeable symbols and, further, relate the two motifs as if the symbols had been fused into one. The result of this synesthetic fusion I take the liberty of calling an "air-prism," though the term is admittedly rather desperate.

Before attempting to explain the air-prism and its functions in *Alastor,* I want to speak of its connection, in this poem and elsewhere, with what some scholars have called Shelley's vision theme.[1] The vision theme is so important for his synesthesia that I shall have to recur to it throughout this study. At the moment it will be enough to refer to one fundamental part of it. This, crudely summarized, is a narrative pattern or structure which tells of a quest for vision on the part of a youthful idealist, the appearance to him of a symbolic "Power" or divinity, his loss or rejection of this vision, and subsequent renewal of the quest. This whole narrative pattern, express or implied, is highly significant for Shelley's use of synesthesia to articulate the meaning of the vision theme; but no part of it better reveals the presence and purport of his synesthesia than passages which describe the coming of the symbolic Power to the visionary.

In such passages, Shelley's descriptive and figurative language is often dominated by certain recurrent and, I feel, easily recognizable motifs, among them being the two already mentioned. For example, Aeolian music and the rainbow are unmistakably associated with a supernal apparition as early as *Queen Mab,* near the opening of which the approach of the Fairy Queen to the dreaming Ianthe is signaled by description of the sound and color that envelop her flying chariot:

> Hark! whence that rushing sound?
> 'Tis like the wondrous strain

That round a lonely ruin swells,
Which, wandering on the echoing shore,
The enthusiast hears at evening:
'Tis softer than the west wind's sigh;
'Tis wilder than the unmeasured notes
Of that strange lyre whose strings
The genii of the breezes sweep:
Those lines of rainbow light
Are like the moonbeams when they fall
Through some cathedral window, but the tints
Are such as may not find
Comparison on earth. (I, 45–58)

These lines present the juxtaposed motifs distinctly and emphatically. Aural and visual aspects are developed in neat sequence, Aeolian music first, and then rainbow light, and each aspect is stressed by repetition. Both of course are meant to suggest visionary ethereality and evanescence.

But the passage is not synesthetic, at least not overtly. So far we can suppose at most that, quite early in Shelley's career, rainbow coloring and Aeolian music in juxtaposition had special significance for his vision theme. To understand further what the significance was, or what it developed into, it may help if we examine Shelley's two motifs as particular aspects of a general symbolism of light and harmony. This can be done most conveniently by turning to the *Hymn to Intellectual Beauty,* composed within the year following *Alastor.* It contains the germ of the vision narrative and, as will be seen, resembles *Alastor* in other respects as well. In it we find that light and harmony are the principal and repeatedly twinned symbols of Intellectual Beauty. A few excerpts will illustrate this sufficiently:

It visits with inconstant glance
Each human heart and countenance;
Like hues and harmonies of evening,—
Like clouds in starlight widely spread,—
Like memory of music fled. . . . (6–10)

Thy light alone—like mist o'er mountains driven,
Or music by the night-wind sent
Through strings of some still instrument,
Or moonlight on a midnight stream,
Gives grace and truth to life's unquiet dream.
(32–36)

. . . there is a harmony
In autumn, and a lustre in its sky,
Which through the summer is not heard or seen. . . .
(74–76)

What Shelley primarily wishes to convey in the *Hymn* is that Intellectual Beauty can be perceived only fleetingly and indirectly. For his imagery and symbolism he therefore prefers light that is mirrored (by moon or streams, for example), veiled (by clouds or mist), or refracted (in water spray), and sounds that, analogously though even more elusively, echo a pure harmony (as in memory) or attenuate it. The drift of all this is clear. It is meant to suggest through forms of light and harmony that a single spirit of beauty and truth may be glimpsed in phenomenal variety. And it is this concern of Shelley's with latent unity which helps to explain why rainbow coloring and Aeolian music, as members of the two image-symbol families of light and sound, play specially significant roles in his vision theme. The colors of the rainbow are not merely varieties of light; their prismatic refraction inevitably stresses their source in unity. But what, then, of Aeolian music? I hope to prove that Shelley fancied an analogy between the prism and the wind harp, supposing that Aeolian sounds testify to a source in unity (some silent *spiritus* of nature) in the way that the spectrum recalls unbroken, colorless light. If we assume this for the moment, we can see that the two motifs would be similarly adaptable to a visionary concern with intimations of the One in the Many, and for this reason alone would be peculiarly attractive to Shelley. But if the rainbow and Aeolian music hint in analogous ways at a latent unity, they likewise imply a transcendence of sensory divisions, or at least an ultimate oneness of light and harmony. What follows, therefore, is that these twin image-symbol motifs invite synesthetic comparison or interchange, and so would afford Shelley an extreme refinement of his attempts to express unity in variety.

For such visionary ends, Shelley must have felt that he could scarcely choose more tractable or acceptable means than those permitted by these favorite motifs. As we have seen, the analogy between colors and music, given Newton's prestige and Castel's prestidigitation, had been all the rage in the eighteenth century. It had been kept fresh, or so one would imagine, by Darwin's "Melody of Colours," and as recently as 1813, Mme. de Staël, in *De l'Allemagne,* was still treating the analogy as a particularly striking evidence of universal correspondences. In short, no aspect of synesthesia ought to have been better known or, in a way, more "respectable" than the parallel between music and rainbow colors. And on the musical side, it should be specially noted, Shelley's Aeolian imagery and symbolism may be said to have gained additional plausibility by equating with nature's colors a harmony that was likewise "natural."

From all this one might conclude that any schematic equation of light and sound, or colors and music, ought to be apparent enough in *Alastor,* if it really does form part of Shelley's visionary construction. That, quite otherwise, the synesthetic scheme has eluded detection is owing in great measure, I believe, to the poet's extraordinary way of combining the two motifs with the analogy between the prism and the Aeolian harp. The analogy, of course, constitutes the basis for the air-prism device and must be discussed further as an additional preliminary to direct treatment of the poem.

II

The analogy is mainly important in Shelley's vision theme as a symbolic means of suggesting the quality and range of perception of his young idealists. We should see nothing very novel or difficult in this, perhaps, if their perception did not, as it does, include synesthetic responses. For fairly unambiguous guidance we can turn once again to *Queen Mab.* At the opening of Part VI Shelley describes the effects of the Fairy's speaking on the disembodied Spirit of Ianthe:

> All touch, all eye, all ear,
> The Spirit felt the Fairy's burning speech.
> O'er the thin texture of its frame,
> The varying periods painted changing glows,
> As on a summer even,
> When soul-enfolding music floats around,
> The stainless mirror of the lake
> Re-images the eastern gloom,

Mingling convulsively its purple hues
With sunset's burnished gold. (VI, 1–10)

Ianthe is not simply blushing. It will be recalled from the Introduction that the phrase "spirit's ear and eye," in *The Retrospect,* seemed to require the reading *ear-and-eye* in order to indicate the source for an implied correspondence between the visible and the audible. Here, although the full meaning of the conceit "All touch, all eye, all ear" will probably forever defy satisfactory explanation, it certainly does not mean that the Spirit is only very attentive, as when we say that someone is "all ears." What Shelley has in mind derives from a passage in Pliny's *Natural History* (quoted in a note to another part of *Queen Mab*) which speculates on the kind of sensibility that would have to be ascribed to deity.[2] But a similar passage of Milton's on suprahuman perception provides a more serviceable gloss. In *Paradise Lost,* Milton writes of

Spirits that live throughout
Vital in every part, not as frail man
In Entrails, Heart or Head, Liver or Reins . . . :
All Heart they live, all Head, all Eye, all Ear,
All Intellect, all Sense. (VI, 344–346, 350–351)

Ianthe similarly is at once all touch, all eye, all ear, and the rest of the passage makes it plain that in this state she *reflects* the *colors* of Mab's speech as a lake reflects the colors of sunset. (I strongly suspect that Shelley, in addition to all else, is punning on the "colors" of rhetoric, but that is quite incidental.) In brief, then, this passage from *Queen Mab* implies a vision psychology which definitely, if still somewhat mysteriously, includes synesthetic perception.

But if Ianthe is synesthetic, Shelley must soon have recognized that his expression of her visionary powers was too crudely and confusingly supernatural. What he required to develop this aspect of his vision theme was to make his synesthetic agent or medium not a disembodied spirit, but a person whose refinement of perception, while possibly approaching the supranormal, remained essentially human. To do this he needed the help of a symbol, or a set of symbols, to characterize the synesthetic agent and express the spiritual implications of that agent's sensory experience. The symbols he chose were the prism and the Aeolian harp, but it is likely that his skill in adapting them to an expression of synesthetic awareness grew slowly and uncertainly. Even in *Alastor*, where he boldly fuses the symbols into the air-prism, Shelley still to some extent appears to find the wind harp a generally more manageable and evocative symbol than the prism. In what follows, therefore, it will be convenient to proceed for a while as though the Aeolian harp, taken to signify both general human perceptiveness and special synesthetic awareness, were the primary development of his effort to discover a symbolic substitute for Ianthe's disembodied spirit.

As a symbol of general human responsiveness to natural and spiritual impulses, or of sympathetic attunement to various "harmonies," the Aeolian harp is of course a frequent property of Shelley's writing, as it is of much Romantic literature.[3] His use of it to express philosophical themes of universal correspondence and all-pervasive harmony is well known and has precedents reaching back to the first imaginative exploitation of the instrument in Thomson's *Castle of Indolence* (1748).[4] But his special association of the harp and its music, or of various Aeolian equivalents, with intersense analogy has gone unremarked.

In verses of Shelley which are found in Claire Clairmont's journal for August–November, 1814, and which their first editor, N. I. White, thought were studies for *Alastor*, there occurs the following fragment:

> Now the dark bows [sic] of the aeolian pine
> Swing to the sweeping wind, and the light clouds
> And the blue sky beyond, so deep and still
> Commingles [sic] like a sympathy of sight
> With the sweet music.[5]

Here the so-called "sympathy" between the visible and the audible gives a valuable clue to the association between Aeolian music and intersense analogy which may be said to form the basis of the synesthetic scheme of *Alastor*. Another quotation, though from a poem written after *Alastor*, goes even further toward proving how greatly Shelley valued and favored this linking of Aeolian and synesthetic strains. Taken from *The Woodman and the Nightingale*, an unfinished poem of 1818,[6] it appears in a context which describes a nymph-haunted forest, full of flowers and pools. The atmosphere of the place is religious and is pervaded by

> the mute
> Persuasion of unkindled melodies,
>
> Odours and gleams and murmurs, which the lute
> Of the blind pilot-spirit of the blast
> Stirs as it sails, now grave and now acute,
>
> Wakening the leaves and waves, ere it has passed
> To such brief unison as on the brain
> One tone, which never can recur, has cast,
> One accent never to return again. (59–67)

The unheard melodies here are a synesthetic unison of "Odours and gleams and murmurs," stirred or awakened by the wind, and since they issue from its "lute," the wind must be considered Aeolian as well as synesthetic. In its elaborate, if somewhat obscure, manner the passage sharply emphasizes the boldness and complexity with which Shelley could exploit the Aeolian harp as a symbol of both natural and synesthetic harmonies.

This broad association between Aeolian and synesthetic motifs can be taken to underlie the special synesthetic connection of Aeolian music with prismatic coloring, and so we are brought back to consideration of the harp-prism analogy. This analogy was not original with Shelley. It was first conceived by William Jones, an eighteenth-century divine, who tried about thirty years after Thomson's literary introduction of the Aeolian harp to explain the "wonderful effect" of this instrument by principles "founded on the analogy between light and air." [7] His curious, pseudo-scientific explanation is clearly one more evidence of the diverse influence of Newton's *Opticks*. As might be expected, Jones's "hypothesis for the solution of Eolian sound" rests on the general belief that "as colours are produced by similar refractions of the rays of light, so musical sounds are produced by similar refractions of the air." [8] Supporting this general equivalence by reference to Newton's spectrum-gamut parallel, and noting that the "analogy between sounds and colours is very strict," Jones concluded: "Upon the whole, the Eolian harp may be considered as an air-prism, for the physical separation of musical sounds." [9]

Certain points and implications of this eccentric hypothesis deserve emphasis. Plainly enough, Jones's "solution of Eolian sound" combines the famous Newtonian parallel with a superficial analogy between the harp and the prism: as light passes through a prism and is broken into colors, so air sweeps through the Aeolian harp and is "broken" into airs. By thus suggesting that air actually contains musical sounds, as white light incorporates colors, Jones implied that the harp makes Nature's voice audible in a real and not merely a metaphorical sense. Since colors and musical sounds are strictly analogous, moreover, Jones's reasoning leads to the metaphysical implication that Nature is an ultimate unity "refracted" in various "prisms." Some such metaphysical notion, at any rate, probably accounts for Jones's real interest in explaining the "wonderful effect" of the Aeolian harp, for all musical instruments should, on the basis of Newton's parallel, have been thought equally marvelous.

This curiosity has been introduced here for several reasons. First, Jones's hypothesis and its implications afford partially clarifying precedents for Shelley's air-prism scheme, insofar as the latter is based on the harp-prism analogy and evokes a metaphysical theme of unity in variety. Second, it is Jones, of course, who supplies the coinage "air-prism," appropriated and modified here to designate Shelley's synesthetic fusion of the prism and the Aeolian harp. Last, and most important, Jones's ideas will help to demonstrate why Shelley's scheme should be understood to involve more than a simple analogy between the two instruments.

Let us apply Jones's concept of the air-prism (that is, the Aeolian harp) to the so-called harp of Memnon. According to legend, the colossal statue of Memnon was believed to resound musically when touched by rays of the rising sun, and because of this musical response, or because some form of lyre was believed to be involved in producing the sound, the statue was sometimes known as Memnon's harp. Marjorie Nicolson has asserted that this legend gained new significance in the eighteenth century because of the interest in light-sound comparisons that had been aroused by Newton's *Opticks*.[10] It may be noted also that in the eighteenth century, as well as later, "Memnonian" and "Aeolian" were occasionally used as though they were synonymous.[11] Hence it is not farfetched to ask what might have been made of Memnon's harp if regarded in terms of Jones's air-prism.

Since the wonder associated with the legendary harp arose from what seemed to be a paradoxical conversion of light into sound, it would not have been difficult to view Memnon's harp as a sort of prism, but one which "refracted" light as music. Hence this music could have been taken to be the equivalent of prismatic coloring. But such an equivalence is exactly what Jones and others deduced from the belief that the "analogy between sounds and colours is very strict." In other words, the light-music refraction of the Memnonian prism could be regarded simply as a fabulous or symbolic means of vividly emphasizing the analogy between sound and light, or music and colors.

Now it is by this kind of Memnonian interchange *and its converse* that Shelley transmutes the harp-prism analogy into the synesthetic air-prism scheme of *Alastor*.[12] If we found this scheme presented with bald theoretical exactness, we should therefore expect the Aeolian harp, symbolizing a youthful visionary, to be treated as though it were also a harp of Memnon and responded musically to light. And, conversely, we should expect a sort of prism which was capable of responding in light or color to impulses of sound. Actually, of course, the scheme is not articulated quite so neatly and does not seem so perversely arbitrary in the poem. If such were the case, it must have been glaringly apparent long ago. But this theoretical description of the scheme may be kept in mind as the best way of understanding that the synesthetic visionary is symbolized not merely as prism or as Aeolian harp but as a fusion of the two.

Finally, it should be emphasized that the foregoing sketch or scheme of the air-prism device provides only the roughest guide to a phase of a developing and extremely complex technique of literary synesthesia. As already indicated, Shelley began to evolve this technique in the earliest stages of his career. It became subtly and profoundly associated with his most intense imaginative concerns, and he never ceased to refine it. What must be remembered, therefore, is that no part of Shelley's effort to articulate his psychological and philosophical insights need be confused with the literal crudity of such things as Jones's air-prism hypothesis, though they may give faint clues to some details of that effort. For a properly sympathetic approach to the synesthetic experiment in *Alastor,* it would be well to observe that by the time of its writing Shelley may already have entered his discipleship to Dante, and his interest in the reflective harmonies of light and music may suggest, at least, such Dantean passages as the one, devoted to the solar heaven, in which the verse so strangely mingles a mirroring of supernal music with the echoing of rainbow splendors.[13]

III

In *Alastor,* there are really two visionaries to whom the air-prism scheme applies. The more important is the nameless young hero of the narrative proper, which begins at line 50. The other is the author himself, whose invocation (1–49) seems carefully designed to foreshadow a number of details in the hero's quest for knowledge and vision. The invocation is addressed, first, to a "belovèd brotherhood" of natural things, all children of one "great Mother" (1–17), and then directly to this mysterious parent of the "unfathomable world" (18–49). Its dominant theme, like that of the *Hymn to Intellectual Beauty*, concerns a self-searching devotion to this phantasmal divinity. Emphasized throughout, therefore, is Shelley's effort to pierce the veils of reality; and the imagery supports this by suggesting a straining beyond the bounds of ordinary perception. He particularly stresses the uncanny sensation of catching tonal intimations in silence itself: in "solemn midnight's tingling silentness" (7); or "When night makes a weird sound of its own stillness" (30). Despite some Gothic trappings, such as sleeping in charnels to force tales from ghosts, the principal imaginative significance of all this stands clear. Shelley is directing the reader's attention toward a realm of vision in which perception transcends its customary range.

The climax of the invocation occurs when Shelley confesses failure to pierce the veil:

> though ne'er yet
> Thou hast unveiled thy inmost sanctuary,
> Enough from incommunicable dream,
> And twilight phantasms, and deep noon-day thought,
> Has shone within me, that serenely now
> And moveless, as a long-forgotten lyre
> Suspended in the solitary dome
> Of some mysterious and deserted fane,
> I wait thy breath, Great Parent. . . . (37–45)

These lines will recall what has been said of Shelley's vision motifs in passages that introduce the ideal being or divinity. Here light and harmony are associated with the expectation of beholding the "Great Parent." But the association is so presented as to imply that light somehow prepares an Aeolian inspiration in the visionary. The burden of the invocation has been a transcendence of ordinary perception, as illustrated in the paradox of audible silence. Here at the climax, I want to suggest that a silent harmony of ideal light may be said to be potentially "refrangible" as Aeolian music. If this holds, the author is symbolizing himself not only as an Aeolian instrument but also as an air-prism.

The hero of the narrative resembles the author of the invocation in almost all except one essential respect, and his preparation for vision is like Shelley's writ large. An introductory lament tells us that he has been a poet, emphasis being laid on his having been a source of music: "Silence, too enamoured of that voice,/ Locks its mute music in her rugged cell" (65–66). In his early career, "Every sight/ And sound" (68–69) combined with historical lore, fable, and philosophy to imbue him with a sacred thirst for truth. As Shelley in the invocation said of the "Mother of this unfathomable world" that he had "watched . . . the darkness of her steps" (18–21), so we learn of the hero that "Nature's most secret steps/ He like her shadow has pursued" (81–82). He traveled across strange landscapes and visited the ruins of early civilizations—Athens, Tyre, Jerusalem, Babylon. In Ethiopia he pored over mysterious figures and symbols in brass and stone, "mute thoughts on the mute walls around" (120). And as Shelley had kept midnight watches in order to compel a message from the great silence, so the young hero studied "those speechless shapes" (123) through day and night. Eventually, such study enabled him to learn "thrilling secrets of the birth of time" (128). All this carries the hero's spiritual career to the point represented in the climax of the invocation. The difference between the hero and Shelley is that the former is not content to remain passive at this point.

Having at first, as Shelley's preface tells us, directed his spiritual quest toward all that is "infinite and unmeasured," [14] the hero lives happy and tranquil, though solitary. When he at length wearies of his solitude, he seeks intercourse not with an ordinary human companion but with an unattainable ideal. This ideal is a projection of all that is best in himself, a "soul out of his soul" or epipsyche, as Shelley would later have termed such a conception, and his search for its antitype amounts to an attempt to comprehend the infinite in a finite embodiment. It is this error, together with a self-centered neglect of others, which exposes him to punishment by the demonic Alastor of the title. Unlike the author of the invocation, therefore, the hero presses his search for vision to a fatal extreme, and his difference is emphasized by an exaggeration of his synesthetic powers.

The ideal projection takes the form of a veiled maiden and comes to him in a dream (151ff). In terms of the image-symbol patterns which appear in the invocation, the transgressing hero will now imagine that he truly hears that "Great Parent's" voice which Shelley only aspired to hear. Hence it is important to realize that the veiled maiden is an Aeolian figure: her speech is a natural music, and her Aeolian significance is stressed in the detail of her having a "strange harp." [15] She appears while the poet sleeps in the vale of Cashmire:

He dreamed a veilèd maid
Sate near him, talking in low solemn tones.
Her voice was like the voice of his own soul
Heard in the calm of thought; its music long,
Like woven sounds of streams and breezes, held
His inmost sense suspended in its web
Of many-coloured woof and shifting hues.
(151–157)

In this, perhaps the most striking passage of the poem, Shelley concentrates the essence of the image-symbol motifs which are under investigation. The music of the dream-apparition, which is like the voice of the hero's soul, is compared to a natural harmony. But this Aeolian music weaves for his visionary hearing a "web/ Of many-coloured woof and shifting hues," and the web presumably is rainbowlike. Apparently, then, this conversion of the music into colors can be ascribed best to the working of the same Memnonian principle by which the author of the invocation hoped to "hear" the ideal illumination which might shine within him. Here the effect is reversed, since it appears that the hero must be conceived as a sort of prism which refracts Aeolian music into colors. Later it will be seen that the hero is also capable of the complementary synesthetic conversion which the air-prism device implies.

The foregoing passage is designedly the most vivid of its kind in the poem. Shelley's *Alastor* version of the vision narrative requires that at this point the hero should be obsessed with the seeming reality and fatal attractiveness of the apparition. In the rest of the story, the hero, while vainly seeking an embodiment of his dream, is denied even a renewal of the apparition in its original completeness and clarity. It is appropriate, therefore, that this anticlimactic aspect of the narrative should be paralleled in the descriptive and figurative motifs. Hence the image-symbol components of the vision motifs are more compactly and unmistakably given here than they are in the narrative sequel. But though this image-symbol scheme does not again appear so brilliantly as here, the motifs definitely are sustained to the end of the poem.

The narrative of the hero's futile search, in which he wanders westward from India to the scene of his eventual death, is an extended allegory that has long defied a wholly satisfactory interpretation,[16] but one aspect of it seems clear enough. In the story of the hero's preparation for vision, his travels obviously were amid spiritual landscapes, not to any geographical Thebes or Cashmire. After the apparition, he journeys across plains and through forests, but these likewise are in countries of the mind. This is especially evident of a rivulet that he follows to the death scene: "O stream!" he cries, "Thou imagest my life" (502 and 505). Hence the allegory sometimes requires that certain images and symbols must be found not in direct application to the hero but in descriptive projections. It is particularly noteworthy, for example, that his onward course is associated with passage through successive arches or canopies of rainbows. In this the many-colored music of his vision must have a powerful influence (though one may assume that the rainbow remains essentially a symbol of an ideal beyond the ideal maiden). In his perplexity after first feeling the loss of the apparition, the hero wonders whether "the bright arch of rainbow clouds" (213) can lead only to disillusion. Later, sailing in a strange shallop, he passes beneath a rainbow canopy which the evening sun has "hung" in the sea spray (333–336). The most impressive example of this sort of allegorical projection occurs in the description of rainbow effects which are created by vine blossoms woven into forest "canopies" above the poet's path (438–451).

The same sort of projection helps to emphasize his symbolic identification with Aeolian instruments, more direct expression of which will be given shortly. In one case, Shelley draws an explicit parallel between signs of aging in the hero and certain changes in the passing landscape.

> so from his steps
> Bright flowers departed, and the beautiful shade
> Of the green groves, with all their odorous winds
> And musical motions. (536–539)

When the hero approaches the end of his journey, the Aeolian projection becomes severe and stark: a single pine hangs over a void and mingles its "solemn song" with "The thunder and the hiss of homeless streams," which are scattered by the wind as they fall into the abyss (561–570).

These projections of the motifs should be interpreted as not wholly coordinated aspects of the hero's ideal, indicating the confusion of his visionary quest; for their basic combination or harmony in the hero himself is more than once made evident. When he is about to die, for example, we learn that his "form" will

> Scatter its music on the unfeeling storm,
> And to the damp leaves and blue cavern mould,
> Nurses of rainbow flowers and branching moss,
> Commit [its] colours. (597–600)

This combination of the motifs is stressed again in a passage that laments his death:

> those hues

> Are gone, and those divinest lineaments,
> Worn by the senseless wind, shall live alone
> In the frail pauses of this simple strain.
> (703–706)

Understanding such uses of the motifs prepares us to detect less obvious geminations. One instance is especially noteworthy for a pun on the word "spectral." Shelley is describing the early stages of the hero's physical and spiritual decline. The wind sings "dirges" in the Aeolian poet's "scattered hair," and the "lustre" of his life begins to fade (248–254). But the desperate ardor of his search is still awesome. To mountaineers who encounter him, he seems a "spectral form . . . the Spirit of the wind" (259). Though ghostly, therefore, his Aeolian spirit keeps its rainbow aspect. Another instance is considerably disguised, involving a blending of light and music in water. Toward the end of the poem, a series of epithets characterizes the dead hero:

> A fragile lute, on whose harmonious strings
> The breath of heaven did wander—a bright stream
> Once fed with many-voicèd waves—a dream
> Of youth, which night and time have quenched for ever,
> Still, dark, and dry. . . . (667–671)

The syntactical arrangement here generally underscores a weaving together of images and symbols, but it should be observed that the "bright stream" includes both an echo ("many-voicèd waves") of the lute's Aeolian music and a suggestion of the light that, in connection with the hero, is often associated with the colors of the spectrum. And since the radiant and sounding stream symbolizes the hero, it may have been intended as a variant or reminder of the air-prism device.

These combinations of the motifs certainly reinforce the contention that the hero is symbolized throughout the poem not merely as an Aeolian instrument but also, and analogously, as a prism. So far, however, we have seen no repetition of the synesthetic Memnonian conversion which this doubling implies. Two more conversions of this kind appear after the dream-apparition, executed in a comparatively restrained fashion, but sufficient reminders, nonetheless, of the hero's being a synesthetic medium. The first is found in a somewhat obscure passage (469–492). The hero, having paused by a fountain in a forest, becomes aware of the presence of a "Spirit" (479). Since this Spirit should most likely be identified with the "Great Parent" of Shelley's invocation,[17] it appears that at this point the hero is being offered an opportunity to escape his obsession with the veiled maiden. But despite a brief communion with the Spirit, he soon reverts to his fixation. It is the form of this communion that requires special notice here. The Spirit, unlike the veiled maiden, never takes definite shape, but reveals itself through "speech" (486) which is composed of

> undulating woods, and silent well,
> And leaping rivulet, and evening gloom
> Now deepening the dark shades. . . .
> (484–486)[18]

In these lines, "*silent* well" helps to stress that the hero is "hearing" in a Memnonian fashion. And the parallel between the hero's relationship to the Spirit and Shelley's to the "great Mother" may be taken to support the likelihood that once again the air-prism device has been brought into play.

The second of these Memnonian conversions is more

easily perceived. The relevant passage deals with the hero's last moments of consciousness:

Yet a little, ere it fled,
Did he resign his high and holy soul
To images of the majestic past,
That paused within his passive being now,
Like winds that bear sweet music, when they breathe
Through some dim latticed chamber. (627–632)

Plainly, the hero's "passive being" is an Aeolian instrument. His "majestic past" should probably be construed as the period before he came under the spell of the veiled maiden, when he was still able to direct his desires toward the "infinite and unmeasured" and to remain "joyous, and tranquil, and self-possessed." [19] Hence the "images" that appear to him now may be associated with that unbounded Power of which the maiden was but a finite semblance. And these images are converted into music-bearing winds as they stream through the air-prism of the hero's soul.

In summary, it should be observed that images and symbols of light and harmony have the same dominant roles in Shelley's presentation of vision motifs in *Alastor* that they have in the *Hymn to Intellectual Beauty* and in comparable parts of other ideal poems. In *Alastor*, too, rainbow coloring and Aeolian music are employed as special aspects of visionary light and harmony in ways that are characteristically Shelleyan. The particular importance of *Alastor* from the viewpoint of this study is that, just as this poem gives the first of Shelley's imaginatively detailed and intricate treatments of the vision narrative, so also it is his first attempt to develop an elaborate synesthetic pattern as an essential element of that narrative. The central device of this synesthetic pattern is the air-prism, designed especially to express a height of visionary awareness in the nameless hero. With his "frame [uniquely] attuned/ To beauty" (287–288), the hero, like Shelley himself in the invocation, is symbolized most obviously perhaps as an Aeolian instrument; but his synesthetic perception requires that his symbolic identity include his being an air-prism.

What needs final remark about the use of this synesthetic scheme within the vision framework of *Alastor* is the extent to which the symbolic relationships and fusions of the air-prism enhance the organic integrity of the poem. A tracing of Aeolian and rainbow motifs is particularly helpful in this connection. These motifs relate primarily to the ideal character of the poet-hero, but through him they are intimately associated both with a supernal Power and with the apparition which resembles that Power. Furthermore, the Memnonian convertibility of the motifs points up the peculiar psychological and philosophical rapport which exists between the hero and his ideal influences. In short, the air-prism device uses intersense harmony to illustrate profound reaches of insight within a theme that deals fundamentally with the apprehension of a single, all-pervasive harmony. Such a theme demands a vehicle which will support its organic complexity, and in *Alastor* it is the synesthetic concept of the air-prism which most notably implies and realizes the fusion of superficially disparate descriptive, figurative, and symbolic strains.

3

MELODY OF LIGHT

I

After *Alastor*, Shelley's synesthesia must be studied with almost exclusive reference to what I am calling the Venus complex, an intricate system of themes, imagery, and symbolism, which dominates his work from 1817 until the end. Scholars so far have done it only piecemeal justice. While I hope to promote its investigation by concentrating on its synesthetic aspects, I ask indulgence if from time to time my restricted topic appears overshadowed by the greater. This is unavoidable, for synesthetic parts of the system compel attention to neglected or little known features of the whole.

The focus of the Venus complex is that planet which we pre-eminently name *the* morning and evening star. Yeats first hailed it in a seminal essay on Shelley: "The most important, the most precise of all Shelley's symbols, the one he uses with the fullest knowledge of its meaning, is the Morning and Evening Star. . . . There is hardly indeed a poem of any length in which one does not find it as a symbol of love, or liberty, or wisdom, or beauty, or of some other expression of that Intellectual Beauty which was to Shelley's mind the central power of the world; and to its faint and fleeting light he offers up all desires. . . ." [1] It focuses also every synesthetic scheme that Shelley developed in and after *The Revolt of Islam,* the earliest among those poems "of any length" which Yeats cites.

As the Introduction briefly states, to understand synesthetic aspects of the Venus complex we must realize that Shelley's purposes led him to write frequently as though certain Pythagorean and Ptolemaic notions were still credible. Adopting the Ptolemaic conception which placed earth at the core of the universe and ensphered it in a series of crystalline heavens, Shelley restored the planet or "star" of Venus to its old position in the third heaven, or sphere, of the series (counting from earth outward). Along with this ancient position, Shelley also gave Venus a Pythagorean harmony. According to Pythagorean tradition, turnings of the transparent, contiguous spheres produced wonderful music, all-pervasive but rarely heard by "grosse unpurged ear." [2] Shakespeare's Lorenzo, in *The Merchant of Venice,* imagines that like music issues from each heavenly body: "There's not the smallest orb which thou behold'st/ But in his motion like an angel sings." [3] Shelley imagines something similar of Venus. All this is commonplace enough. Shelley's brilliant innovation, the basis of many synesthetic refinements, lets intersensory perception symbolize the rare spiritual elevation needed to hear this mystical harmony. In other words, he makes Venus's light synesthetically audible. And then, going further, he establishes the converse of this by making ethereal harmony perceptibly radiant.

This synesthetic combination of light and harmony in connection with Venus is discernible in two short quotations. In a passage of *The Triumph of Life,* Shelley calls the following a "wonder" worthy of Dante:

> The world can hear not the sweet notes that move
> The sphere whose light is melody to lovers. (478–479)

The "sphere," as A. C. Bradley and others have observed, is the third, Venus's the "light." [4] Hence these lines distinguish from the gross "world" those "lovers," devotees of a heavenly Venus, who synesthetically hear supernal melody in her light. The second quotation shows pretty much the converse. In one fragment connected with *Epipsychidion,* Shelley warns interpreters of love poems like his:

> let them guess
> How Diotima, the wise prophetess,
> Instructed the instructor, and why he
> Rebuked the infant spirit of melody
> On Agathon's sweet lips, which as he spoke
> Was as the lovely star when morn has broke
> The roof of darkness, in the golden dawn,
> Half-hidden, and yet beautiful.[5]

This recalls that part of Plato's *Symposium* in which Socrates tells how Diotima instructed him about the highest love, about Uranian, as opposed to Pandemian, Aphrodite.[6] Agathon, a dramatic poet, had preceded Socrates in praising love, and the philosopher reproved him for speaking more eloquently than truthfully. In these lines, Agathon's lyricism is styled "infant spirit of melody," because presumably it would grow into still nobler strains under direction of Socrates.[7] But its melody was anyway lovely enough to resemble light of the morning star. Hence this and the first quotation signify that Venus's light and music are synesthetically equivalent.

This equivalence and related matters will be examined in this chapter mainly as they appear in *The Revolt of Islam, To a Skylark,* and *The Triumph of Life*. In *The Revolt* basic elements of the Venus complex emerge in broad outline, and synesthetic interrelationships among some of them are plainly evident. *The Skylark* reveals how Shelley equates ethereal lark song with spheral music and with Venus's light. In *The Triumph of Life* one can see how synesthetic designs help to clarify the poem's fundamental conflict between a Uranian and a Pandemian Venus.

II

Venus, the most brilliant planet, must have appeared especially conspicuous to Shelley during the summer of 1817, his last in England. A year later, writing from the Bagni di Lucca to his friend Peacock, he playfully recalled how Venus had impressed him: ". . . the nights are forever serene, and we see a star in the east at sunset—I think it is Jupiter—almost as fine as Venus was last summer; but it wants a certain silver and aerial radiance, and soft yet piercing splendour, which belongs, I suppose to the latter planet by virtue of its at once divine and female nature. I have forgotten to ask the ladies if Jupiter produces on them the same effect."[8] In 1817, from March to September, Shelley worked steadily on *The Revolt of Islam,* made therein his first major draft on the resources of the Venus complex, and one way or another must have kept the planet continuously in view. It appears in *The Revolt* as both morning star (Lucifer or Phosphor) and evening (Vesper or Hesper); and both phases of it symbolize related themes of love and liberty.

Longest of Shelley's poems (twelve cantos, more than 500 Spenserian stanzas), *The Revolt* is a modern epic of a struggle for social, political, and religious freedom—a contest which Shelley likened to a beau ideal of the French Revolution. In a letter to Byron he spoke of its being written "in the style and for the same object as 'Queen Mab,' but interwoven with a story of human passion, and composed with more attention to the refinement and accuracy of language, and the connexion of its parts." [9] As this comparison suggests, he wished *The Revolt* to have a large audience, but its style is hardly popular. He himself conceded that "if it were all written in the manner of the first canto, I could not expect that it would be interesting to any great number of people." [10] The first canto is an allegory and, as Shelley said, may be regarded to some extent as an independent poem; but while the rest tells what he called "a mere human story," [11] it has levels of meaning to which the first canto is a needed introduction. In fact, despite Shelley's popular ambitions (or designs), the whole of *The Revolt* seems dauntingly akin to his "visionary rhymes."

This kinship has advantages for reading later "ideal" poems, because *The Revolt* does after all resemble *Queen Mab* in point of style. Superficially, at least, expression is usually simple and direct; and this, together with a sort of epic expansiveness, familiarizes us with thematic groupings of images and symbols which Shelley later handles with pronounced obliquity and concision.

Expansiveness is particularly evident in his using the entire first canto as introduction. The allegory describes a fight between an eagle and a serpent, which respectively represent forces of evil and good. The power of good, though in serpent guise, is primarily identified as the maligned Morning Star (Lucifer) of human hopes. Its contest with the eagle, symbol of religious and political tyranny, is only the latest in an age-old series in which the good, though ever resurgent, appears forever baffled by superior strength. After defeat on this occasion, the serpent falls into the sea but is rescued by a beautiful, mysterious woman. Then the narrator, witness of both struggle and rescue, embarks with the woman and serpent on a marvelous voyage to a celestial "Temple of the Spirit," where is recounted the history of Laon and Cythna, protagonists of the main narrative.

In this poem Shelley has inverted the values of the supposedly Hebraic Lucifer-serpent symbol and endued it with a strong Promethean cast. The Morning Star's Promethean fire is especially emphasized when Shelley describes the role of ancient Greece in the long battle against powers of darkness:

Then Greece arose, and to its bards and sages,
In dream, the golden-pinioned Genii came,
Even where they slept amid the night of ages
Steeping their hearts in the divinest flame
Which thy breath kindled, Power of holiest name!
And oft in cycles since, when darkness gave
New weapons to thy foe, their sunlike fame
Upon the combat shone—a light to save,
Like Paradise spread forth beyond the shadowy grave.
(I, xxxii)

Light and fire of this Prometheus-Lucifer play throughout the rest of the poem, because the Morning Star recurrently influences the action and is personified or reflected in Laon and Cythna, who at the close suffer *their* temporary defeat on a pyre erected by tyrannical forces. Their relationship both to the Morning Star and to one another is anticipated in the first canto by the experience of the beautiful woman vis-à-vis the serpent. The woman is clearly one of Shelley's feminine embodiments of supernal qualities. She sings in an unearthly language, described as the "native tongue" of the Morning Star (I, xix), and "silver sounds" (I, xviii), Shelley's epithet for her strange melody, probably tries to give commonplace phrasing synesthetic and symbolic significance. As native tongue of the Morning Star, that is, "silver sounds" should be construed specifically as planetary harmony. Affinity between the woman and the Morning Star is further disclosed when the narrator likens her to the planet Venus in its evening phase:

> Then she arose, and smiled on me with eyes
> Serene yet sorrowing, like that planet fair,
> While yet the daylight lingereth in the skies
> Which cleaves with arrowy beams the dark-red air.
> (I, xxi, 1–4)

She is Vesper, then, he Lucifer. This doubling of the Venus symbolism modifies the meaning of Shelley's Lucifer in an important way, for we might otherwise suppose him merely a somewhat exalted version of Milton's Satan, a character for whom Shelley, as is well known, expressed qualified admiration. The Lucifer-Vesper, male-female relationship emphasizes that the essential force in Shelley's revolutionary philosophy is love, not hate.

In stanzas xxxv and following of the introduction, the

woman tells her life story. In what is revealed of her lonely dedication and sympathy with nature, she resembles the hero of *Alastor,* though she is otherwise different enough. After rejoicing over the coming of the French Revolution, she had fiery visions of a Spirit which clearly was the Morning Star (I, xl–xliii). Thereafter, she became an active revolutionary, constantly aware of her sustaining spirit in the natural music of woods and waves, and in heavenly lights (I, xlv–xlvi). All this contains hints of the air-prism scheme, but intersense analogies are not used to express her visionary experience. Just before the voyage to the Temple of the Spirit, which concludes the introduction, the woman ends her personal narrative on a mysterious note. After many years, she says,

> I was awakened by a shriek of woe;
> And over me a mystic robe was thrown,
> By viewless hands, and a bright Star did glow
> Before my steps—the Snake then met his mortal foe.
> (I, xlvi, 6–9)

(Here, *mortal* primarily means *deadly.*) Then, in the Temple of the Spirit, the narrator tells how the woman faded into supernatural darkness, while the serpent was metamorphosed into a resplendent male personification of the Morning Star. Both of them, presumably, have been absorbed into a single being, which is or represents Venus. At this point Laon and Cythna are introduced, and their "mere human story," a long flashback, follows.

As Laon and Cythna are counterparts of the two allegorical figures, their similarly mysterious intimacy is also, and more often, accentuated by synesthetic interchange. That Laon may be a Lucifer has already been noted by Baker in specific reference to Canto II.[12] Here we learn that Laon wishes to cleanse the world with fire (II, xiv, 5), and he invests his thoughts with "the light/ Of language" (II, xvi, 6–7). Later in the poem his *shouted* name is like "a *bright* ghost from Heaven" (V, vii, 7; emphasis added). In relation to Cythna, Laon appears as a visionary ideal, much as the Morning Star appeared to the Vesperlike woman, and as the veiled maiden to the *Alastor* hero. This becomes plain when Cythna describes her solitary, introspective education, which includes divining lore taught in "old Crotona," and especially when she adds:

sweet melodies
Of love, in that lorn solitude I caught
From mine own voice in dream, when thy dear eyes
Shone through my sleep, and did that utterance harmonize.
(VII, xxxii, 6–9)

"Harmonize" may often have very general significance, of course, but here it synesthetically keys a complex expression. In view of Laon's role as Lucifer and Cythna's mention of lore of Crotona, where Pythagoras reputedly taught, "harmonize" probably refers to spheral music, which was supposed to "attune" virtuous spirits. Light from Laon-Lucifer's eyes, especially since it harmonizes a love song, can readily be associated with the light of Venus. Cythna's song, then, has been attuned to a "melody of light," Shelley's synesthetic equivalent of spheral music. All this resembles what we found in *Alastor* and suggests that Shelley here has superimposed the melody-of-light scheme upon his air-prism device.

That Cythna is a Venus in her own right becomes clear at another point in the story. Shelley partly makes this identification by having Laon speak what is really an adaptation of a Platonic epigram. His speech shows that just as he is a Lucifer to Cythna, so (according to this version of the Greek)[13] she is to him a "Fair star of life and love" (IX, xxxvi, 5). Laon tells her this after she has made a long, inspired speech; she ends after nightfall, but,

> Though she had ceased, her countenance uplifted
> To Heaven, still spake, with solemn glory bright.
> (IX, xxxvi, 1–2)[14]

Here Cythna's emergence as a kind of Vesper, evening "star . . . of love," seems obvious. The sense transfer involved in a bright face speaking, while in itself banal, adds to the evidence that this is a duplication of the reciprocal relationship between the Morning Star and the woman of the introduction.[15]

The main narrative also echoes and amplifies other aspects of the relationship between the two allegorical figures, most notably perhaps in Canto VI. There Laon tells how his revolutionary forces suffer a disastrous rout, from which Cythna rescues him. After escaping on a giant black horse, they take refuge in the cavernous hall of a marble ruin, situated on a mountain overlooking the sea. The general circumstances of this rescue and flight recall the events which followed the Morning Star's defeat by the eagle; and minor details reinforce this broad parallel. For example, both serpent and Laon finally succumb at evening; again, as the woman conducts the serpent in a boat with "prow of thin *moonstone*," so the horse on which Cythna carries off Laon has its front marked with a "white moon" (I, xxiii, 2; VI, xxvi, 3). Symbolically, these details imply that during the night of defeat the spirit of good survives in the light of the evening star and the moon.

At the close of Canto I, fusion of two meteoric lights

into "One clear and mighty planet" (I, lvi, 7) appears to represent the union, in the Temple of the Spirit, of Venus's Lucifer and Vesper phases. For Laon and Cythna in Canto VI, the cavernous hall is a similar temple, and becomes the scene of their nuptial union. Hall and nuptials are both described symbolically. The hall is domed with clinging vegetation which, like the forest canopy in *Alastor*, is starred with parasite blooms; and its leaves and flowers give rise to Aeolian music (VI, xxvii–xxviii). This reprise of the Aeolian-rainbow motifs develops in successive stanzas (VI, xxix-xxx), which respectively liken Cythna and Laon's love to ideal harmony and supernal light; and the two motifs enter again with the sudden appearance of a Meteor (a Venusian surrogate?), which symbolically blesses the marriage. The Meteor hovers in the dome while Aeolian music sounds through leaves; the light is "wondrous," the sound like that "of a spirit's tongue" (VI, xxxii).

This familiar combination of ideal light and music, three times repeated here, prepares for Shelley's attempt, in five stanzas that anticipate the ardent lyricism of *Epipsychidion*, to depict a perfect mingling of bodies and souls. In *Epipsychidion*, as will be seen, Shelley carefully associates a harmony of the senses with union of two Venuslike spirits. Most likely, therefore, the two motifs here are meant to ready us for synesthetic expression of this marriage between Laon-Lucifer and Cythna-Vesper. The five stanzas (VI, xxxiii–xxxvii) refer crowdedly to a variety of intense sensations, and the climax of the lovers' communion suggests a fusion of all senses in mystical unity. Laon asks significantly: "Was it one moment that confounded thus/ All thought, all sense, all feeling, into one/ Unutterable power . . . ?" (VI, xxxv, 1–3). But though obviously elaborate and piquantly anticipatory of Shelley's later practice, the synesthetic plotting of these stanzas lacks incisiveness.

In contriving synesthetic links among aspects of the Venus complex, Shelley perhaps deliberately confined himself to commonplace or easily construed imagery. But on at least one occasion in *The Revolt* he ventured a synesthetic figure which presages later intricacies. Partly based on the poem's symbolic coupling of liberty with light and fire, this figure involves light-sound comparison with the shouted name of liberty itself. The comparison is deceptive, both in its leisurely unfolding and in use of water as a medium, but at its close the whole figure is shot with meaning by a single adjective. In Canto IX, an astonishing cry of *Liberty!* is heard by thousands gathered on seaside cliffs:

> As o'er the mountains of the earth
> From peak to peak leap on the beams of Morning's birth:
>
> So from that cry over the boundless hills
> Sudden was caught one universal sound,
> Like a volcano's voice, whose thunder fills
> Remotest skies,—such glorious madness found
> A path through human hearts with stream which drowned
> Its struggling fears and cares, dark Custom's brood;
> They knew not whence it came, but felt around
> A wide contagion poured—they called aloud
> On Liberty—that name lived on the sunny flood.
>
> (IX, iii–iv)

Here likeness of sound to a dawn light of liberty is established directly at the beginning. In lines immediately preceding the quotation, the cry is said to rise "Like Earth's own voice" (iii, 5). Now, in this extended image, that association of natural sympathy with moral triumph is picked up thematically: the "universal sound" of Liberty is like "a volcano's voice, whose thunder fills/ Remotest skies"—the volcano's explosive "dawn" being left to imagination. The sound then streams like water, but its light persists, as is intimated by the drowning of *dark* Custom and, with mild punning, by the stream's "*glorious* madness." At the last, the basic analogy swiftly and convincingly re-emphasizes itself through the watery medium. When the multitude respond to that first cry of *Liberty!* and repeat it, the directness of the original equation is partially restored, and the name lives on the echoing "*sunny* flood." The whole passage permits readers to believe that, as an original cry from the sea has reverberated over land, so now an echoing shout from the hills merely resounds over water. But within this literally acceptable construction, Shelley has woven unmistakably symbolic, synesthetic meaning.[16]

III

Of all Shelley's poems, *To a Skylark* (composed in 1820) seems least likely to require synesthetic scholia. Mrs. von Erhardt-Siebold, Firkins, Fogle, and S. C. Wilcox[17] have canvassed its intersense analogies ably and sensitively, and I do not intend to repeat their work. But in certain synesthetic images none of them has unsealed what Shelley's very concise language holds by virtue of his Venus symbolism.

The heart of the poem, from my special point of view, lies in two stanzas, the fourth and fifth, and my remarks will deal almost entirely with them. These stanzas, so annoying to T. S. Eliot,[18] read:

The pale purple even
Melts around thy flight;
Like a star of Heaven,
In the broad daylight
Thou art unseen, but yet I hear thy shrill delight,

Keen as are the arrows
Of that silver sphere,
Whose intense lamp narrows
In the white dawn clear
Until we hardly see—we feel that it is there.

Eliot was annoyed principally because he could not identify the "silver sphere" and felt confused by the reference to "white dawn," following upon "purple even" (and "broad daylight" as well, presumably). Shelley scholars are usually unembarrassed to identify the sphere as Venus; I do not know that any have tried to account for the seemingly jumbled references to time. In both matters, however one may reply to Eliot's charge that Shelley has here given "sound . . . without sense," [19] I believe his critical instinct was penetrating, for his remarks suggest, not really that Shelley wrote inanely, but rather that a good deal of sense here must elude the ordinary reader. As he put it, "Shelley should have provided notes." [20]

That the sphere (planet, not Ptolemaic sphere) is Venus has been asserted most effectively on astronomical grounds by Housman, authoritative in such matters, and by A. Eiloart on grounds of familiarity with Shelley's symbolism.[21] For the latter the best gloss is a passage of *The Triumph of Life* (lines 412–419) where Shelley describes the morning star ("Lucifer") waning at dawn until it is *felt*, though *unseen*. I have no doubt that the identification is correct and want now to give additional evidence for it—evidence which will also bear on the references to dawn, daytime, and evening.

In these two stanzas Shelley obviously took pains to stress how similarly the lark disappears in early evening sky and the morning star gradually fades at dawn. Once lost to view, each continues to affect the poet. The planet remains there in the morning sky, of course, and he somehow feels its influence. (That is the case at least if we follow the gloss from *The Triumph of Life*; in *To a Skylark* Shelley's "hardly see" suggests deliberate ambiguity about transition from seeing to feeling.) Likewise, the lark hides in the sky like a star during the daytime, but its song reaches hearing. This similarity supports the synesthetic comparison of the second stanza: the sustained influence of the star-lark, its song, equals the continued presence or influence of the morning star; that is, some awareness that the planet's light, though obscured by the sun, is still there. In this sense, then, the lark's song is like Venus's light. But, in addition, once having allowed that the radiant song synesthetically resembles planetary brilliance, I think we see where Shelley is heading. The lark differs from stars by being lost in early evening sky, not in "broad daylight." Now, among stars that evening restores, first to appear is Vesper, just as Lucifer fades last in the morning. And since the lark's song synesthetically equals Venus's light, Shelley has in effect placed a Vesper in the evening sky. Hence the two stanzas tightly and logically show that the lark is a kind of Venus.

This must have seemed a happy, exciting invention to Shelley and may seem so to readers acquainted with the body of his poetry. I am not sure what a common reader attending to the *Skylark* in isolation would make of it. But, thinking of Shelley's concern in and beyond this poem with a whole system of imagery and symbolism, I believe it is interesting and pertinent to speculate on the background of this lark-Venus identification.

In verse of the 1817–1818 period, Shelley quite remarkably tries to describe the song of nightingales synesthetically. Insofar as these descriptions go beyond sound-light analogies, in order to bring in references to other sense data, I want to reserve certain of their synesthetic aspects for discussion in the next chapter. Here I would simply point out, first, that the synesthetic descriptions clearly mean to accentuate mystical qualities in the nightingales' singing, and, second, that it looks as though Shelley wants to identify their singing with spheral music. The first point scarcely needs argument if the descriptions are taken in their contexts. In the highly "ideal" *Prince Athanase* (composed in 1817), a nightingale's song "overflows in notes of liquid gladness/ Filling the sky like light!" (lines 201–202). In *Rosalind and Helen* (composed in 1817–1818), a long passage (lines 1102–1186) of this designedly popular but occasionally visionary poem makes a nightingale's very synesthetic song preside over the ideal union of Helen and Lionel and seem to awaken human emulation in Helen's singing and harp playing. (This recalls Crashaw's great synesthetic virtuoso piece, *Music's Duel,* in which nightingale and lute player enter into rivalry; comparison hurts Shelley sorely.) Finally, in *The Woodman and the Nightingale* (possibly composed in 1818),[22] from which a complex synesthetic passage has already been quoted in the previous chapter, a nightingale's song, repeatedly and variously synesthetic, is described throughout as an ideally harmonizing power.

The second point—that the nightingale's singing is a spheral music, or its naturally audible equivalent—may be argued best from the last of these poems. But in all three

Shelley specially associates the song with sky or heaven. The example from *Prince Athanase* speaks for itself. In *Rosalind and Helen,* the bird flies in an evening sky, and we learn that its song is "heaven-resounding minstrelsy"—in fact a "heaven-taught tale." In *The Woodman and the Nightingale,* the song rings and shines through the whole world of the night, including "every sphere," "the abyss/ Of Heaven with all its planets," and its effect on everything, except one rough woodman, is precisely that which the traditional Pythagorean harmony supposedly worked on all susceptible matter and spirit.

If this second point holds up, an interesting synesthetic, symbolic connection appears between the song of nightingales and the melody of Venus's light. Through synesthesia, both—the light wholly, the song partly—represent spheral music. Given a set of synesthetic equations like this (a equals x, b equals x), Shelley seldom left untested the axiomatic conclusion (a equals b). Now, even if the *Skylark* lacked the fourth and fifth stanzas, its similarity to *The Woodman and the Nightingale,* synesthetically and otherwise, would immediately suggest that the lark, like the nightingale, audibly echoed spheral music in singing "from Heaven, or near it" (first stanza). In the fourth and fifth stanzas, the lark is temporarily or incidentally a Vesper; for the whole poem it chiefly represents spheral music in general, not the special melody of Venus's third sphere. Logically, I believe, Shelley thought first of the lark as he did of his nightingales, taking its song only as spheral music, and then afterward saw his nice opportunity to identify its song with Venus's melody. When he had done so, he had, in addition to all else, endowed this melody with a splendidly actual voice.

One last point may be in order regarding this association

of lark and nightingale with the spheres. Shelley probably made it with a hint from Milton in mind. His well-known devotion to that poet and his imaginative interest in Pythagorean harmony render it most unlikely that he could have missed the following in Milton's academic prolusion, *De sphaerarum concentu:* "Why, credible it is that the lark itself should fly right up to the clouds at early dawn, and that the nightingale should spend the whole lonely night in song in order that they may adjust their strains to the harmonic mode of the sky, to which they listen attentively." [23]

IV

To examine the synesthesia of *The Triumph of Life* (composed in 1822), I take for basis the reference to Venus's melody of light and the passage on Dante in which it occurs (471–80). Though everyone would agree that *The Triumph of Life* is Shelley's most Dantesque poem, the Dante passage has never been properly related to the rest of this difficult, magnificent fragment (in terza rima, it breaks off just short of 550 lines). Usually passed over as digression or incidental tribute, its chief relevance to the rest lies in its connection with the Venus complex. The fragment as a whole (so to speak) presents the conflict between a Uranian and a Pandemian Venus, and emphasizes oppositions between their respective lights and sounds. The Dante passage, sanctioning one side, celebrates spiritual, heavenly love and associates its influence with the melody of Venus's light. Both the synesthesia and the general theme of the passage are highly significant for the entire fragment.

My over-all interpretation of the poem agrees with that of most Shelley scholars, but calling the opposed figures higher and lower Venuses needs special comment. One figure, a "Shape all light," most commentators accept as a feminine embodiment of ideal qualities and term generally "Divine Beauty," "Spirit of Intellectual Beauty," "Imagination," "Love," and so on.[24] Specifically, Baker named her Iris, goddess of the rainbow; Grabo thought her possibly Uranian Venus; Yeats said repeatedly and emphatically that she was the morning star.[25] In my opinion, a proper reading will validate Yeats's identification. The other figure is also a "Shape," but an evil one. At line 180, she seems to be called "Life," and I think it satisfactory to take her as the titular Life. Yet much indicates her equation with a Pandemian Venus, as my special approach may help to show. Most important is her very opposition to the other, Uranian Shape. (In this connection it is well to insist on the breadth of Shelley's Venus symbolism here and elsewhere: to call Life a Pandemian Venus in no way "reduces" her significance.) But there are still other reasons to believe that Life had definite Venus associations for Shelley. As Baker has demonstrated, Life strikingly resembles Spenser's Lucifera and her pageant in *The Faerie Queene*;[26] and the name Lucifera could be no trifling matter to Shelley. Regarding influences, moreover, Bradley has argued that of Petrarch's six *Trionfi*, with which everyone links *The Triumph of Life*, "Shelley owes little to the last five . . . but a good deal to the first"—namely, to the *Triumph of Love*.[27] Still, though many scholars subordinate a lower Venus, a "fierce Spirit," to Shelley's Life,[28] only Peter Butter, to my knowledge, has called the evil Shape itself Pandemian and asserted unequivocally that the fragment has for theme a distinction between the higher and the lower Venus.[29] I am going to agree with him.

The general structure of the fragment has been divided aptly into a prologue and three sections.[30] The prologue (lines 1–40) discovers the author at dawn looking westward to sea from "the steep/ Of a green Apennine" (probably part of the Ligurian Apennines); having been awake through the night, he now falls into a visionary trance. What he beholds occupies all three sections. Section one (41–175) shows an immense stream of people hurrying along "a public way." Representative of every age, they are the conquered in the triumphal progress of Life, who rides in a chariot from which emanates a "blinding light." Section two (176–300) introduces Rousseau, himself captive, who comments to the narrator on Life's almost universal victory over the great in every sphere of human endeavor. In section three (300–548), Rousseau first tells his own life story in idealized fashion, emphasizing his vision of the "Shape all light" and his subsequent self-betrayal to Life; he then comments anew, with great vividness, on the essential causes and consequences of spiritual failure among Life's victims.

According to this division, the Dante passage falls in section three. Rousseau has been describing himself as one among the captives, dragging through a wilderness after the chariot. Then:

> Before the chariot had begun to climb
> The opposing steep of that mysterious dell,
> Behold a wonder worthy of the rhyme
>
> Of him who from the lowest depths of hell,
> Through every paradise and through all glory,
> Love led serene, and who returned to tell

The words of hate and awe; the wondrous story
How all things are transfigured except Love;
For deaf as is a sea, which wrath makes hoary,

The world can hear not the sweet notes that move
The sphere whose light is melody to lovers—
A wonder worthy of his rhyme.

Here one must recognize clearly that more than one "wonder" is referred to. There are at least three. One (471) appears in the *Inferno*-like narrative which follows this passage, telling how shadows and veils of evil obscure Life's victims. To this the second use of the word (480) again looks forward; but it also marks the sort of Dantesque wonder which Shelley has just illustrated—that is, the synesthetic melody of Venus's third sphere. The third wonder ("wondrous story," 475) concerns Dante's conception of "How all things are transfigured except Love" (476). This third may be said to include the other two, even though these are metamorphic opposites. The first refers to sinister transfigurations; the second (synesthetic interchange of Venus's light and melody) transfiguratively hints at an ideal unity behind appearances.

Why is the second, synesthetic wonder called worthy of Dante? One might suppose that Shelley simply alludes to the fact that, in *Paradise*, Cantos VIII and IX, the third sphere teems with spirits described as singing and speaking lights—for example, "The light . . . , which was yet strange to me, continued from out of its depth where it was singing before" (IX, 22–23).[31] But since Dante does not distinguish the third sphere from others in this respect, Shelley much more likely evokes Dante's own use of synesthetic expression. It will be shown presently that a well-known sense transposition of *Inferno* (it occurs twice) had already been adapted by Shelley in a passage that precedes the Dante one. My main contention here hardly needs support of specific citations like this, however. The whole Dante passage reveals persuasively enough what might otherwise be taken for granted—that Shelley of all readers enjoyed supreme qualifications to penetrate the subtle, philosophical intent of Dante's synesthesia.

As already indicated, the really comprehensive wonder alluded to (and it has importance for the whole of *The Triumph of Life*) is that "wondrous story/ How all things are transfigured except Love." This marvel of Dante's art and metaphysics is described best in awesome lines near the end of *The Divine Comedy*, when he attempts to give some notion of the beatific vision: "O abounding grace, by which I dared to fix my look on the Eternal Light so long that I spent all my sight upon it! In its depth I saw that it contained, bound by love in one volume, that which is scattered in leaves through the universe, substance and accidents and their relations as it were fused together in such a way that what I tell of is a simple light" (*Par.*, XXXIII, 82–90). Love's fusion of all substances and accidents into the ineffable unity of *un semplice lume* provides for Dante the ultimate philosophical rationale of synesthetic expression used throughout *The Divine Comedy*, but increasingly in *Purgatory* and *Paradise*. He lets a progressively developing sensitivity to intersense analogies parallel spiritual purgation and elevation, and brings all at last to this flaming sum of things. Shelley, it may be, was the first to comprehend this. Once we are acquainted with it, at any rate, his Dante passage speaks volumes. Specifically, regarding synesthetic aspects of the Venus complex in *The Triumph of Life*, the passage intimates that only "lovers," not the gross "world," can hear the melody of light, can understand how all things are transfigurable except a divine Love.

In all three sections of *The Triumph of Life,* imagery and symbolism are dominated by an opposition between lights and sounds, belonging to the opposed Venuses, which encompasses the melody-of-light scheme. This can be discerned most plainly in Rousseau's narrative in sections two and three. Discovered by the narrator among the "deluded crew" about Life's dazzling chariot, Rousseau laments that,

> if the spark with which Heaven lit my spirit
> Had been with purer nutriment supplied,
>
> Corruption would not now thus much inherit
> Of what was once Rousseau. (201–204)

Then he tells how renowned historical personalities fared in their battles with life's corruptions, all of them having been defeated and darkened by a fatal lack of self-knowledge (208–215). Rousseau, in this, elaborates on the theme of Shelley, qua narrator, though the latter had exempted at least a "sacred few"—eagles of the divine flame who escaped earthly exile to return to their "native noon" (128–131). Rousseau includes even Plato among the conquered:

> The star that ruled his doom was far too fair,
>
> And life, where long that flower of Heaven grew not,
> Conquered that heart by love, which gold, or pain,
> Or age, or sloth, or slavery could subdue not.
> (256–259)

Here "star" and "flower" refer to Aster, a youth rumored to have infatuated Plato. Aster is addressed as both morning and evening star in the supposedly Platonic epigram which Shelley translated and took as motto for *Adonais,* and which illuminates star symbolism in that poem. Obviously a Venus in the epigram, Aster here is both star and flower (the implied pun has long been noted)[32] of *love,* and Rousseau transparently implies that, if Plato fell, his subduer represented Pandemian Venus.

Rousseau at length describes his own infidelity to an ideal, Uranian Venus. The opening portion of his confession recalls the story of the *Alastor* hero. He says that in "the April prime" (308) or morning of life, he had been laid asleep under a mountain through which flowed a Lethean stream. While he still slept, the spell of the stream's music was so "sweet and deep" that it rendered him forever oblivious to his previous existence. When he awoke,

> for a space
> The scene of woods and waters seemed to keep,
>
> Though it was now broad day, a gentle trace
> Of light diviner than the common sun
> Sheds on the common earth, and all the place
>
> Was filled with magic sounds woven into one
> Oblivious melody, confusing sense
> Amid the gliding waves and shadows dun. (335–342)

Vestigial divine light in the "broad day" may be from Venus. The "magic sounds" are natural, Aeolian. Both light and sounds, confusing Rousseau's "sense," prepare him for the coming vision of the Uranian Shape. Looking toward the cavern, which one must visualize as piercing quite through the mountain and arching over the stream, Rousseau sees the sun's image burning on the water. Within the blazing sun stands the ideal Shape:

> A Shape all light, which with one hand did fling
> Dew on the earth, as if she were the dawn,
> And the invisible rain did ever sing

A silver music on the mossy lawn;
And still before me on the dusky grass,
Iris her many-coloured scarf had drawn. (352–357)

Shelley here combines light and music in a single emanation—the dew flung down by the Shape both creating "silver music" and taking on rainbow colors. Hence Rousseau's Shape appears to that double accompaniment of prismatic color and natural music which repeatedly marks the presence of ideal figures in Shelley's poetry. Except for the slightly suggestive "silver music," no intersense analogies support the scheme, but the familiar twin motifs hint at what is intended and what follows. The synesthetic intent, along with the Shape's crucial identification, is manifest in a passage which Rousseau now devotes to telling how his ideal vision faded and the "new vision" (411) of Life replaced it. Though long, the passage must be quoted entire:

> And the fair shape waned in the coming light,
> As veil by veil the silent splendour drops
> From Lucifer, amid the chrysolite
>
> Of sunrise, ere it tinge the mountain-tops;
> And as the presence of that fairest planet,
> Although unseen, is felt by one who hopes
>
> That his day's path may end as he began it,
> In that star's smile, whose light is like the scent
> Of a jonquil when evening breezes fan it,
>
> Or the soft note in which his dear lament
> The Brescian shepherd breathes, or the caress
> That turned his weary slumber to content;
>
> So knew I in that light's severe excess
> The presence of that Shape which on the stream
> Moved, as I moved along the wilderness,

More dimly than a day-appearing dream,
The ghost of a forgotten form of sleep;
A light of heaven, whose half-extinguished beam

Through the sick day in which we wake to weep
Glimmers, for ever sought, for ever lost;
So did that shape its obscure tenour keep

Beside my path, as silent as a ghost;
But the new Vision, and the cold bright car,
With solemn speed and stunning music, crossed

The forest, and as if from some dread war
Triumphantly returning, the loud million
Fiercely extolled the fortune of her star.

Much invites comment here, for symbolically, at least, the passage is the most revelatory in the whole fragment. And all is not obvious. What *is* obvious is that the passage clinches Yeats's identification of the Shape as Venus and my assertion that the Dante passage best guides our understanding of how Rousseau relates to this ideal figure. Rousseau proves he had once known Venus's melody of light, but confesses his present deafness to it. Instead, he hears only too well the contrasting "stunning music" of another star (438). And "star" hardly seems inadvertent if Shelley wants us to realize that his Uranian star opposes a Pandemian. Astronomically, the Pandemian star may be impenetrably mysterious. The Uranian is mysterious, too, but yields clues. Rousseau, speaking of "his day's path" (418), reveals that he had beheld Venus in the morning of life and that one can hope, though perhaps *he* does not, to see and hear it again at evening. Now, to speak so implies that Venus is morning and evening star on one and the same day and compels us to imagine that its movement parallels the sun's, but invisibly, of course, except at dawn and twilight. In nature the facts are quite different: Lucifer and Vesper never share the same day. But this stylization of Venus's movement eminently suits Shelley's vision theme: it permits his linking a youthful, visionary perception of an ideal to observation of Venus at dawn; loss of the vision has its equivalent in Lucifer's waning; feeling that the vision, though lost, still exerts some influence is like the feeling that Venus, though unseen, remains above; hope that the vision will return in full glory, when common daylight has faded, takes inspiration from the hope of again observing Venus as Vesper.

This stylization, we can now see, was already implied in the fourth and fifth stanzas of the *Skylark*. In the ode we may imagine that Shelley, hearing the lark's radiant, Venus-like song at evening, proclaims a triumphant reappearance of the star after "broad daylight." It is like realizing the hope, expressed in the other of his two most famous odes, that the west wind's "azure sister of the Spring" will come when winter passes. And we shall see that Shelley had used similar stylization before *The Triumph of Life* in *Adonais*, where Keats as Lucifer passes through temporary eclipse to emerge as immortal Vesper.

Three synesthetic similes in the passage help to define the quality of visionary response to light of the third sphere. Light of the star is like the scent of star-shaped jonquil (419–420). It is like a Brescian song (421–422), and this, like the jonquil comparison, may have more than synesthetic appropriateness. A note of Mary Shelley's says that the poet had a specific song in mind, "a Brescian national air."[33] Brescia was a Lombard province, then enduring Austrian rule but famous for its resistance to tyranny, and a *national* "lament" inevitably reminds one of revolutionary aspiration in this particular melody of light. Finally, the light is like a caress (422–423). All three mean to prove that Rousseau customarily heard what the "world" never hears.

But these similes do not exhaust synesthetic expression in the passage. Two epithets, which have escaped comment, concisely reinforce the significance that the melody of light has, or should have, for Rousseau. First of these is "*silent* splendour" (413). Unobtrusively, but perhaps disastrously, this announces Rousseau's deafness to the melody of light. This kind of negative intersense analogy, perfectly adapted to Shelley's aims here, appears twice in Dante's *Inferno,* and I have no doubt that Shelley emulates his master. In *Inferno,* Canto I, Dante tells how, driven back by a wolf into the "dark wood" of sin, he returned "to where the sun is silent" (line 60). Again, in Canto V, he says of entering the circle of the lustful, "I came to a place where all light was mute" (28). In both instances he implies that divine grace irradiates audibly, thus combining the Gospel's *verbum* and *lux.* (So, e.g., in *Purgatory,* XXXIII, 75, Beatrice's word is a dazzling light.) Shelley's usage recalls this. "Silent splendour," applied to Lucifer's light, would be absurd if not taken to mean that Rousseau has suffered spiritual aphasia. The second epithet is "obscure tenour" (432). Superficially, it refers to the Shape's unobserved course in following Rousseau's path—a westward path, incidentally, going with the stream that flows away from the morning sun. But it appears meaningful also as the converse of silent splendor. It involves a pun, which I find not at all unusual in Shelley's synesthetic expression. Keeping her hidden way beside Rousseau, the Shape resembles Venus in that sunlike journey across the sky which Shelley has invented for her. And although unheard, she resembles the planet in holding her high melody (tenor deriving from Latin *tenere* and signifying both a general course of conduct and a musically high range). The first epithet stressed silencing of ideal light; "obscure tenour" stresses darkening or hiding of ideal harmony. Hence Rousseau is synesthetically and spiritually blind as well as deaf. In the way of the "world," he sees and hears well enough the splendor and music of the Pandemian star.

Negative synesthesia in the epithets suggests that as the melody-of-light scheme relates to the Uranian Venus, a contrasting scheme may relate to the Pandemian. So far as images or figurative motifs are concerned, this does not appear with great force, though the lower Venus's "icy cold" brilliance is insisted on (77, 78, 434). Nevertheless, there are clear indications that Shelley meant Rousseau's spiritual deafness to be balanced by symbolic "deafness" to the glaring Pandemian light. This appears in section one and the beginning of section two.

In first describing Life's triumphal progress, the narrator, *not* Rousseau, says:

So came a chariot on the *silent storm*
Of its own rushing *splendour.* (86–87; emphases added)

Unlike Rousseau, the narrator seems never to hear—not to heed, at least—the "stunning music" that comes from the conqueror's chariot. Shelley emphasizes that he hears only wing-beats of the "wonder-wingèd team" which draws it along (95–98). Later he observes a Bacchanalian crowd of captives dancing wildly to the "savage music" (138–175), and Rousseau urges him not to join the agonized dance (188–189). At first, therefore, the narrator seems to be exempt: the stormy splendor is silent. Afterwards, if he hears the corrupting music, he remains deaf to it in the sense that he can, as Rousseau admits he could not, forbear joining the tempestuous dance. Evidently, then, the "silent . . . splendour" of the Pandemian balances the symbolically contrary "silent splendour" of the Uranian Venus. This symbolic ambivalence perhaps deserves to be underscored. Lovers of the higher Venus are attuned to an ideal, spheral harmony and synesthetically "hear" it in the planet's light. So attuned, they are "deaf" to the Pandemian's garish splendor. Devotees of the latter have never heard ideal strains or have lost the faculty of hearing them. At best, Uranian light is to them a silent splendor. At worst, they are wholly possessed by the Pandemian's maddening music, dazzled by her freezing glare.

V

For convenience of exposition, its immense aid in probing the Venus complex, I have taken *The Triumph of Life* somewhat drastically out of chronological order, especially by associating it with *The Revolt of Islam.* Inconveniently, this obscures trends of Shelley's synesthetic art toward the close of his career. What we find in *The Triumph of Life,* and in *Adonais* shortly enough before, indicates interestingly divergent developments. On the one hand, individual synesthetic images become as a rule increasingly subtle (as in "silent splendour" and "obscure tenour") and allusive (as in comparing Venus's light to the jonquil's odor and to the Brescian song). On the other hand, Shelley's synesthetic schemes, as schemes, lie increasingly open to detection, particularly because (as in the Dante passage) he so plainly signals their relationship to Venus symbolism. All this may be explained generally by his growing poetic skill and confidence. But if compared with *Prometheus Unbound* and *Epipsychidion, The Triumph of Life* may appear synesthetically firmer, sharper, even lovelier, mainly because it is so much simpler.

4

EPIPSYCHIDION: THE EMBODIED RAY

I

IN *Epipsychidion,* composed early in 1821, Shelley's personal or "confessional" expression of his vision theme reaches its greatest development. The poem is frankly, though somewhat riddlingly, autobiographical—"an idealized history of my life and feelings," as Shelley told a correspondent.[1] As history, it has a distinct air of finality, and in writing it Shelley seems to have been thoroughly conscious of his opportunity to give one portion of his work its definitive handling. The spiritual union with Emily (Emilia Viviani), which it chiefly celebrates and which represents the limit of his personal aspiration toward the ideal, is described with extraordinary assurance. Not least remarkable about its style, peculiarly rich even for Shelley, are the frequency and variety of intersense analogies. Whereas *The Triumph of Life* mainly compares data of sound and sight only, manipulated according to the fairly simple melody-of-light scheme, *Epipsychidion* attempts much denser synesthetic notation, striving for marked inclusiveness of sense referents generally, as well as for complex expression of their interrelationships. In this effort, and in connection with Venus symbolism, Shelley exploits such interchanges of spheral light and music as were examined in the last chapter; but the melody-of-light scheme, narrowly interpreted at least, comes far short of accounting for the comprehensive synesthesia here.

This principally involves Shelley's attempts to create an acceptable source of multiple synesthesia, by which I mean either of two things, though it is not always easy to distinguish between them in his practice. One source sends out a single sensory emanation (the light of Venus, let us say), which synesthetically affects several senses. Thus, in *The Triumph of Life,* Venus's light is not only musical but is also comparable to the scent of a jonquil and to a caress. The other is a source, or what one may imagine to be a source, of several sensory emanations (sound, light, odor, and so on), all of which may have synesthetic effects, or somehow relate to one another synesthetically. It is the latter that Shelley tries to create in the "embodied rays" of *Epipsychidion,* though the term may suggest the simpler sort. But before discussing this further, I want to illustrate something of his earlier experiments with such sources.

Experiment with the simpler kind is observable in the synesthetic nightingales of 1817–1818, already noted in the previous chapter. In *Rosalind and Helen,* the nightingale's "bright and liquid" song resembles primarily, if not very vividly, an intoxicating wine (1118–1120; 1129–1130). But is is also likened to odor, in daringly elliptical fashion:

suddenly
'Tis scattered in a thousand notes,

And now to the hushed ear it floats
Like field smells known in infancy. (1107–1110)

In *The Woodman and the Nightingale,* the song of the bird is said to

Satiate the hungry dark with melody;—
And as a vale is watered by a flood,

Or as the moonlight fills the open sky
Struggling with darkness—as a tuberose
Peoples some Indian dell with scents which lie

Like clouds above the flower from which they rose,
The singing of that happy nightingale . . .

Was interfused upon the silentness. (5–14)

The intention here seems apparent enough. I would only remark how convincingly the opening line ("Satiate the hungry dark with melody") reveals Shelley's determination to load the nightingale's song with its synesthetic burden.

A more complex, and certainly less clear, source of multiple synesthesia occurs in a long passage of *Lines Written among the Euganean Hills,* composed in 1818. Shelley describes a mysterious noontide mist of light. Its widely diffused glow is

Like a vaporous amethyst,
Or an air-dissolvèd star
Mingling light and fragrance. . . .
(288–290)

As in *The Triumph of Life* and *Adonais,* this star of light and fragrance may involve a pun on the Greek *aster;* and it may be the midday Venus of Shelley's visionary stylization. But its mystical effects are evoked in verses which signify pretty plainly that this curious "solution" basically sends out more than light:

> And of living things each one;
> And my spirit which so long
> Darkened this swift stream of song,—
> Interpenetrated lie
> By the glory of the sky:
> Be it love, light, harmony,
> Odour, or the soul of all
> Which from Heaven like dew doth fall,
> Or the mind which feeds this verse
> Peopling the lone universe. (310–319)

Taken in context, and related to such visionary verse as the *Hymn to Intellectual Beauty,* the entire passage (285–319) seems to me one of Shelley's finest. Synesthetically, it shows strain. It appears to summarize a variety of sensations and thoughts, gathered more from the surrounding landscape than from an "air-dissolvèd star," and to project all into "the glory of the sky." This quite aptly suggests a dazzling simultaneity and exaltation of responses. But the dew-precipitating solution of light, though possibly acquiring symbolic strength from connection with the Venus complex, does not seem a satisfactory source of multiple synesthesia.

Both experiments, with nightingales and the noontide mist of light, show Shelley's general drift toward creating effects of multiple, even a sort of total, synesthesia. More important, they emphasize his determined effort to associate such effects with a single source or medium. And it is precisely the challenge involved in this which he tried to meet by conceiving the embodied rays of *Epipsychidion.*

II

At this point it may be useful to enlarge on what was said of Shelley's concept of the embodied ray in the Introduction, and especially to consider how he may have come to it. As already indicated, the embodied ray is best explained by analogy with the prism. Looking at it in this manner, we can say that the air-prism device of *Alastor*, by which prismatic light interchanges with Aeolian sound, is a kind of two-dimensional anticipation of the embodied ray. In the latter, a supernal light is so refracted as to affect all of the senses, revealing not merely that the refracted "colors" (sound, light, odor, and others) have various synesthetic relationships, but also that they derive from the one light. In response to "beams" of the embodied ray, therefore, the proper sort of seer would compose anew the refracted elements and, while still aware of their prismatic variety, know also the unbroken light. (It will save unnecessary confusion to keep in mind that ordinary light is as much subordinate to the divine illumination as is sound, for example.)

However odd this notion of an embodied ray may seem, it is probably not original with Shelley, at least not in its components. His lifelong concern with rainbow coloring, to say nothing of his synesthetic invention of the air-prism device, sufficiently guarantees that before composing *Epipsychidion* Shelley as reader would have been especially alert to imagery and symbolism of refraction. Hence it is worth noting that two prism figures of the most striking kind can be found in his reading, that they have a nexus in Dante, and that they have extraordinary pertinence to his concept of the embodied ray, since one has only to combine them in order to arrive at it.

In Canto XXV of *Purgatory,* Dante represents himself as being curious to learn how the disembodied spirits of the other world can appear so lifelike. Statius, who has the role of elucidator here, explains that in life each man has three "souls": the vegetative, the sensitive, and the "potential intellect," or true soul. Only the last survives the body after death. In the other world, this soul, by its radiant "virtue," acquires an aerial body (88–90). Its radiation is like that of the sun in vapor: "as the air, when it is full of rain, becomes adorned with various colours through another's beams that are reflected in it, so the neighbouring air sets itself into that form which the soul that stopped there stamps upon it by its power" (91–96). According to Dante, then, the soul is an incarnate ray, its body a vaporlike prism. Although truly a "shade," this aerial body (the soul's "new form" in the quotation that follows) possesses all the functions of sense and, in turn, makes itself perceptible to the senses: "then, like the flame that follows the fire wherever it shifts, its new form follows the spirit. Since it has by this its semblance henceforth, it is called a shade, and by this it then makes organs for every sense, even to sight; by this we speak and by this smile, by this we shed tears and make the sighs thou mayst have heard on the mountain" (97–105).

All of this helps enormously in understanding what Shelley means when he calls Emily "an embodied Ray/ Of the great Brightness." [2] But it tells nothing about the synesthetic aspect of his conception. For this we have a remarkable hint in Mme. de Staël's *Corinne,* which Shelley read in December, 1818, and may have had specially in mind about the time he wrote *Epipsychidion,* since we know that he and Mary lent their copy of it to Emilia Viviani.[3] De Staël's heroine Corinne, herself a poet, says the following of Dante while improvising on the occasion of her being crowned with the laurel at Rome: "The magic words of our greatest poet are the prism of the universe, all of whose wonders reflect themselves in it, divide, and join again; sounds act like colors; colors melt into harmony. . . ."[4] Even in 1818 this passage, combining as it does so many of Shelley's liveliest interests, must have leapt from the page at him. In 1821, he would have found the universal prism of Dante's poetry exactly the sort of *corpus* he sought to embody divine light—one that would refract and at the same time recompose by means of intersense analogies. In any case, taken together with Dante's own extended exposition of the human body as prism, it completes what is necessary for basic understanding of Shelley's embodied ray.

That he thought of so combining materials from Mme. de Staël and Dante is only conjecture, of course. Strictly speaking, he had his own perhaps sufficient model in the air-prism device of *Alastor*. But it seems fair to claim that what he found in these authors, Dante especially, probably encouraged him in an invention which might strike some as the most bizarre fantasy, were no such poetic and philosophic antecedents discoverable. This is not to imply by any means that Shelley's philosophy of the soul agrees with Dante's. Shelley's, in fact, probably approximates the Averroistic thought which Dante's Statius combated—belief that human beings are only perishable manifestations of a universal soul. Thinking of Emily as an incarnate ray of the "great Brightness," one recalls the supposedly Averroistic concept of the universal soul's being "a spiritual radiance broken up, coloured and particularized by the prisms of our bodies."[5] Some such prism figure, no less than the idea behind it, very likely stirred Dante. And the interesting possibility confronts us that Shelley took over details of Dante's figure precisely in order to reassert an Averroistic view.

III

In *Epipsychidion,* there are three main embodied-ray passages, a possible fourth one, and a final glancing but definite recollection of the basic scheme. Singly and collectively, all these passages have far from simple relationships to other elements of the poem, some of which must be taken into rather considerable account here. It will be convenient, therefore, to divide the poem, 604 lines in loose heroic couplets,[6] into six parts—noting first that the text is preceded by a motto which is taken from Dante's canzone addressed to spirits of the third sphere ("Ye who by understanding move the third heaven")[7] and so alerts us to look once again for a development of Shelley's Venus complex. Part I (1–71) apostrophizes Emily herself. Part II (72–123) describes her to the reader as an embodied ray. Part III (123–189) is transitional, apostrophizing Emily again, but chiefly discoursing on the philosophy of love. Part IV (190–387), the heart of the poem, is a vision narrative, the "idealized history of my life and feelings." It proceeds from Shelley's early apprehension of an ideal Being (possibly an embodied ray), through subsequent attempts to find the "shadow" of that Being in "many mortal forms," to the fulfillment of his search in discovering Emily, who in the climax is again presented as an embodied ray. Part V (388–591) invites Emily to escape with Shelley to an enchanted island. This island itself is an embodied ray. Toward the end, Shelley's relationship to Emily is put so as to equate him with her, and make him an embodied ray also. Part VI (592–604) is a brief, Dantesque *envoi.*

Part I abounds in ecstatic epithets which strive vainly to sum up Emily's various glory and beauty. Forms of light and harmony (both natural and human), emotional completions—a "world of fancies" (70)—all fail to express what she essentially is. At length the poet confesses the infirmity of this intense effort (69–71). To appreciate best what he has aimed at here and how he is principally to go on, we must turn to the opening of the vision narrative in Part IV. Here Shelley describes the "Being" or Power of his youthful visionary experiences (190–216). This Being, personified as a feminine spirit, closely resembles the ideal presences of the *Hymn to Intellectual Beauty* and *Alastor,* the inspiring "mind" of *The Euganean Hills,* the stellar Venus and nightingale of various poems. Her influence on his early youth, before fading "Into the dreary cone of our life's shade" (228), is exerted mainly by her "voice," which he divines principally in natural sounds, paradoxically in "all silence," and synesthetically "hears" in

the odours deep
Of flowers, which, like lips murmuring in their sleep
Of the sweet kisses which had lulled them there,
Breathed but of *her* to the enamoured air. (202–205)

Her voice is otherwise more than natural, coming to him in "words/ Of antique verse and high romance," in various forms of art, and in philosophy whose "taste" transfigures mortal existence (209–215). In short: "Her Spirit was the *harmony* of truth" (216, emphasis added). She is never "beheld," being "robed in . . . exceeding glory" (199–

200). Since this "glory" is thus made up of a great variety of appeals to the senses and the mind, Shelley possibly wants us to interpret the Being as a sort of embodied ray, but all this, like the noontide mist of *The Euganean Hills*, seems to lack focus. The important point for the moment, however, is that it tells us enough to appreciate Emily's essential kinship with her both before and after the introduction of the Being.

This kinship and Emily's nature as an embodied ray are best seen in two passages, one in Part II, the other in Part IV, toward the conclusion of the vision narrative. As one further brief preliminary to their examination, it will help to note that these passages, like the rest of the poem, contain much astronomical imagery, and that far from being "scientifically correct," as White argued,[8] this is more Ptolemaic than anything else. It is certainly inconsistent. For example, Shelley's nomenclature makes no distinction between star and planet, which is not unusual in his verse. But one may be surprised indeed to note some of the astronomical transformations he effects here: a Comet is invited to take a less disturbing role in Shelley's universe by becoming "Love's folding-star," Venus (368–374); and Emily, frequently referred to as a star and once as a "Splendour" of the third sphere (116–117), becomes the sun in the poem's climax (321ff.). Hence we should be prepared to observe that in the first of these two passages she is primarily a Venus.

This passage (72–123) is neatly unified by balanced references in its opening and close to cycles of the day, the year, and human life, Emily being respectively morning, spring, and youth. (Paradoxically, however, she is also the peace of "sweet Death.") In the rest of the passage, which will require extensive quotation, she is an embodied ray:

> the brightness
> Of her divinest presence trembles through
> Her limbs, as underneath a cloud of dew
> Embodied in the windless heaven of June
> Amid the splendour-wingèd stars, the Moon
> Burns, inextinguishably beautiful. (77–82)

Following this comes the first synesthetic expression, which indicates that her embodied "brightness" must be connected with spheral music:

> And from her lips, as from a hyacinth full
> Of honey-dew, a liquid murmur drops,
> Killing the sense with passion; sweet as stops
> Of planetary music heard in trance. (83–86)

Now, in lines which strongly recall Statius's exposition for Dante's benefit, Shelley concentrates on expressing (mainly in terms of moving, fiery light) how the soul of Emily shines through her whole presence:

> In her mild lights the starry spirits dance,
> The sunbeams of those wells which ever leap
> Under the lightnings of the soul—too deep
> For the brief fathom-line of thought or sense.
> The glory of her being, issuing thence,
> Stains the dead, blank, cold air with a warm shade
> Of unentangled intermixture, made
> By Love, of light and motion: one intense
> Diffusion, one serene Omnipresence,
> Whose flowing outlines mingle in their flowing,
> Around her cheeks and utmost fingers glowing

With the unintermitted blood, which there
Quivers, (as in a fleece of snow-like air
The crimson pulse of living morning quiver,)
Continuously prolonged, and ending never,
Till they are lost, and in that Beauty furled
Which penetrates and clasps and fills the world.
(87–103)

This "glory," moving with its light and warmth to an accompaniment of spheral music, is also synesthetically fragrant:

Warm fragrance seems to fall from her light dress
And her loose hair; and where some heavy tress
The air of her own speed has disentwined,
The sweetness seems to satiate the faint wind;
And in the soul a wild odour is felt,
Beyond the sense, like fiery dews that melt
Into the bosom of a frozen bud. (105–111)

Commenting on all this as "a precise and detailed formulation of an experience that negates our usual mental distinctions," G. Wilson Knight said, "Something is *made* from all the senses, sight, 'fragrance,' warmth and cold, music, some fluidity of which these are aspects but which to receive as one whole is quite supernormal." [9] This is generally excellent, but it remains to add that the "fluidity" quite clearly emanates from embodied brightness. Even the odor is like "fiery dews"; and when we learn, in lines that belong with those quoted, that Emily is "a Splendour/ Leaving the third sphere pilotless" (116–117), it becomes plain why her synesthetic speech has effects of "planetary music." Such speech is a form of the melody of light. And the manifold synesthetic brightness that irradiates from Emily derives ultimately, in this passage, from the sphere of Venus.

The passage in Part IV which describes Emily as an embodied ray follows the "historical" narrative of Shelley's unsuccessful attempts, before meeting her, to find the Being of his youthful visions in other "mortal forms." It is interesting to note that this Being, like Emily in the first of these two passages, relates variously to Venus. Before her fading, Shelley says, he had tried to fly toward this "lodestar . . . of desire" (219), as a moth might "seek in Hesper's setting sphere/ A radiant death" (222–223). And when she disappears, "like a God throned on a wingèd planet" (226), she passes "Into the dreary cone of our life's shade" (228). Shelley, as we know, repeatedly describes the "shading" of Venus by daylight, and it seems certain that the Being whom he met in "youth's dawn" (192) subsequently passed into the "dreary cone" of life's commonplace day. All of this indicates that the Being, like Emily, we should primarily identify with Venus.

Surprisingly, therefore, the second embodied-ray passage (321–344) describes Emily not as Lucifer or Vesper but as the sun, though this is not entirely clear at first. After his many wanderings, Shelley says, Emily entered the "obscure Forest" of his life and irradiated it with "splendour like the Morn's" (321–324). The first intersense analogy links sound and light, a reminder of the entrancing planetary music in the first passage:

> music from her respiration spread
> Like light,—all other sounds were penetrated
> By the small, still, sweet spirit of that sound,
> So that the savage winds hung mute around.
> (329–332)

Here, too, fragrance and warmth are once more combined:

> odours warm and fresh fell from her hair
> Dissolving the dull cold in the frore air. (333–334)

All this, lightlike breath of music and fiery odor, prepares for the assertion that Emily is an embodied ray:

> Soft as an Incarnation of the Sun,
> When light is changed to love, this glorious One
> Floated into the cavern where I lay,
> And called my Spirit, and the dreaming clay
> Was lifted by the thing that dreamed below
> As smoke by fire, and in her beauty's glow
> I stood, and felt the dawn of my long night
> Was penetrating me with living light. (335–342)

Synesthetically, this passage is less impressive than the earlier one. Though Emily obviously incarnates light, Shelley seems almost content to remind us of what he had established so carefully before, emphasizing now a sort of promotion of Emily to sunlike eminence in a universe which contains Shelley himself as the earth, Mary as moon, and that "beautiful and fierce" Comet, usually supposed to be Claire Clairmont, which is so strangely bidden to return as Vesper, "Love's folding-star" (374). Part IV closes with this nice *consideration.* In the remaining major section, and the longest, Shelley with his highly relativistic astronomical symbolism restores Venus to its usual place of central importance and reveals that the embodied ray belongs mainly to the Venus complex.

IV

Part V, like the last one-third or so of *Adonais,* has sometimes been judged a rather ill-joined addition to a poem which had already once been finished. It is well known that Shelley "ended" *Prometheus Unbound* with Act III and then, some months later, wrote Act IV as an "afterthought"; this has undoubtedly encouraged speculations that he may have acted similarly on other occasions. And several features of *Epipsychidion* do in fact suggest that the first 387 lines (Parts I–IV) present a satisfying whole, with which the rest is autobiographically and logically inconsistent. But any such suggestion in this instance must depend sheerly on internal evidence.

With Emily's apotheosis as incarnation of the sun, Shelley's autobiographical microcosm appears definitively ordered. Following this, moreover, is a short passage (383–387) which distinctly echoes the opening lines of the poem and likens all between to a wreath of song. Then the supposed "addition" invites Emily to elope with Shelley to an Ionian isle and describes this enchanted place at some length. Here, apparently, the lovers will find their home in death as well as for the remainder of their lives. But the projected elopement fails to accommodate the other women who, though heavenly bodies inferior to the sun, distinctly shared the poet's universe. In other words, the end of the poem seemingly ignores, or undoes, the well-regulated world fashioned by the first four parts.[10] Besides this autobiographical contretemps, other evidence of disjunction has been descried in "a contradiction in the thought."[11] In the philosophical Part III, Shelley argues "that love increases through multiplication of the beloved objects," being like light, which "from a thousand prisms and mirrors, fills/ The Universe with glorious beams" (166–167).[12] Hence it is objected that in Part V "not only is the excursion to the dream island contemplated with but one beloved, but the object of this pair of lovers is to get away even from their duality." [13] As Shelley puts it: "We shall become the same, we shall be one/ Spirit within two frames" (573–574).

To the latter objection I would reply that Shelley's title (*Epipsychidion:* soul within the soul, or soul out of the soul), together with the over-all logic of the poem's vision narrative, militates strongly against it. The Being of his youthful visions was a "soul out of my soul" (238), and Shelley wished to be absorbed in its radiance, like a moth consumed in flame (220–224). But Emily, in whom that Being is realized, must be the titular epipsyche, and his pursuit of her aims at self-annihilating union. Already in Part I, in fact, Shelley announces to Emily, "I am not thine: I am a part of *thee*" (52; Shelley's emphasis). In short, they are somehow one by the very nature of his epipsychic discourse. So, too, I believe, the autobiographical objection loses cogency if we view the elopement in light of the vision theme. Its narrative logic, imagery, and symbolism indicate that on the whole Emily's relationship to the Venuslike Being of Shelley's early experience takes precedence over her relationship, as temporary sun, to moon, comet, and so on. And it is exactly the greater relationship which Part V returns to and underscores.

The island where the eloping lovers might find haven, though variously described, is clearly supernatural. It is really that world of which Emilia Viviani herself wrote, in words Shelley placed before his "Advertisement" to the poem: "L'anima amante si slancia fuori del creato, e si crea nell' infinito un Mondo tutto per essa, diverso assai da questo oscuro e pauroso baratro" (The loving soul launches itself beyond creation, and creates for itself in the infinite a World wholly its own, much different from this dark and dreadful abyss).[14] Although Shelley says that the island rests under an Ionian sky, "Beautiful as a wreck of Paradise" (422–423), yet no keel has ever ploughed a path to it (411). Any actual location in the Aegean can be merely incidental to its true nature:

> It is an isle 'twixt Heaven, Air, Earth, and Sea,
> Cradled, and hung in clear tranquillity;
> Bright as that wandering Eden Lucifer,
> Washed by the soft blue Oceans of young air.
> (457–460)

This "Lucifer" is in fact another incarnation of Venus, of that lodestar of desire to which the youthful visionary wished to fly, the starry Being which attracted him as Hesper might draw a moth. While the moth seeks "radiant death," and while Shelley says that Emily "lured me towards sweet Death" (73), it is entirely appropriate to the argument of *Epipsychidion,* by which the poet finds a mortal embodiment of his vision, that arrival at this island Venus should be imagined to take place before death. But, then, "life" and "death" tend to exchange their customary meanings in Shelley's verse, and we shall find that, if annihilation of personality after death becomes a merging with the island's "soul," so "life" on the island is scarcely less than such death.

Not only a Lucifer, the island is also an embodied ray:

> Yet, like a buried lamp, a Soul no less
> Burns in the heart of this delicious isle,

An atom of th' Eternal, whose own smile
Unfolds itself, and may be felt, not seen
O'er the gray rocks, blue waves, and forests green,
Filling their bare and void interstices. (477–482)

"Felt, not seen," like the Venus of *To a Skylark* and *The Triumph of Life*, this emanation of divine light transmits a synesthetic harmony, according to an earlier passage on the supposedly natural beauties of the island:

And all the place is peopled with sweet airs;
The light clear element which the isle wears
Is heavy with the scent of lemon-flowers,
Which floats like mist laden with unseen showers,
And falls upon the eyelids like faint sleep;
And from the moss violets and jonquils peep,
And dart their arrowy odour through the brain
Till you might faint with that delicious pain.
And every motion, odour, beam, and tone,
With that deep music is in unison:
Which is a soul within the soul. (445–455)

Since we have often observed that spheral or Venusian harmony and light are interchangeable, I take it that this effluent, multiply synesthetic music should be understood as a melody of light, issuing from the island's lamplike soul. The island, then, emerges as essentially an embodied ray; and the "smile" of the Eternal (479) produces a harmony which, equivalent to supernal illumination, is synesthetically "refrangible." This recalls, of course, the simpler Memnonian conversions of *Alastor*, as the island landscape generally recalls the multiply synesthetic mist of *Lines Written among the Euganean Hills*. As another prism of multiple synesthesia, the island, in addition to being one more Venus with the Being and Emily, complements the embodied-ray imagery and symbolism of Parts II and IV.

The line quoted last above (455) deserves special note for its reference to Shelley's title and its explicit echo of the Being's identification within the threefold epipsychic pattern: the Being was "this soul out of my soul" (238). The island further resembles the Being by association with various aesthetic and philosophic ideals: thoughts and joys, "Folded within their own eternity" (524). Hence Part V clinches a logical return to the foundations of Shelley's visions—that is, to detailed apprehension of ideal presences in nature and the human spirit. One important difference is that life on the island sustains uninterrupted communion with the ideal, whereas the Being's visitations were truly sporadic; and this alone should convince us that the elopement really represents visionary ascent, rather than autistic desertion. As the poem works toward its finale, life on the island marks one stage in progress toward union with the eternal; perfect union with Emily ensues; and at last, in death, the lovers merge with the island's soul.

This visionary progression, moving logically from the Being's appearance in Shelley's youth to his absorption after death in the soul of the island, implies that Emily's celebration subserves a more comprehensive theme, much as elegy gives way to eulogy of the One in *Adonais*. Emily's apotheosis as the sun in Part IV, as already indicated, climaxes only a single movement, a kind of epicycle in the astronomical symbolism of the whole, and should not obscure the primary pattern of Venus references. This nowise detracts from Emily's importance as the poem's subject. Human image of a bright eternity (115), she but transiently embodies divine brightness; yet she principally focuses Shelley's celebration precisely because, in her humanity, she most intensely realizes the ideal. In time, she best confirms the possibility of communion with the eternal.

The concluding lines of Part V (540–591) stress Emily's role in lifting Shelley to her own plane, revealing that he too may be a kind of Venus. The poet's perspective changes from that of fortunate seer of the ideal to that of equal participant in radiant elevation. By virtue of the poem's extraordinarily relativistic astronomy, he becomes a meteor, twin to a meteoric Emily (576); and the subsequent complete or nearly complete fusion of the two points to their essential Venusian identity, which, again, would be indistinguishable in death from the regnant stellar symbol of the whole work. It is remarkable, therefore, that the lines which present Shelley altered from seer to participant relate subtly to the first description of Emily as an embodied ray, in Part II. When the poet asserted earlier, "Love makes all things equal" (126), he was praying rather than pronouncing. Now the prayer seems answered. In the first embodied-ray passage, Emily's glory emanated from *wells* which lay "Under the lightnings of the soul" (89), beyond fathoming of thought or sense. Now description of the lovers' perfect union echoes the earlier conception:

> the wells
> Which boil under our being's inmost cells,
> The fountains of our deepest life, shall be
> Confused in Passion's golden purity.
> (568–571)

A passage shortly preceding this symbolizes conversation between the lovers by paradoxes which demonstrate mutual, rather than unilateral, influence and leave no doubt that Shelley will affect Emily as she had affected him:

> And we will talk, until thought's melody
> Become too sweet for utterance, and it die
> In words, to live again in looks, which dart
> With thrilling tone into the voiceless heart,
> Harmonizing silence without a sound.
> (560–564)

This unheard melody of thought, which lives in the tone of looks and harmonizes silence, should be related to Emily's "planetary music heard in trance" in the first embodied-ray passage, and probably also to the harmony, heard in "all silence," of the Hesperian Being. If we recall the dominant Venus symbolism of the poem, and note particularly that the two lovers, merged like twin meteors, will become the "living soul" of the island Venus (539), I believe their one silent melody of thought must incontrovertibly range with music of the third sphere. And all this, though put in language of two senses only, suggests well enough that Shelley, too, is to be an embodied ray. The final slight, but sufficient and self-explanatory, confirmation comes in description of the lovers' merger:

> We shall become the same, we shall be one
> Spirit within two frames, oh! wherefore two?
> One passion in twin-hearts, which grows and grew,
> Till like two meteors of expanding flame,
> Those spheres instinct with it become the same,
> Touch, mingle, are transfigured; ever still
> Burning, yet ever inconsumable:
> In one another's substance finding food,

Like flames too pure and light and unimbued
To nourish their bright lives with baser prey.
(573–582)

V

Throughout this chapter I have not hesitated to say or imply that the Being *is* Hesperian; that Emily, as a splendor of the third sphere, *is* a Venus; that the island *is* a Lucifer; and lastly that Shelley also *is* a meteoric Venusian counterpart of Emily. To those who are familiar with the oblique practices that characterize much of Shelley's later ideal poetry, this will not seem misleading or unjustifiable. As will be seen, for example, *Adonais* invites us not only to seize on more or less abstruse allusions, but also to trace obscure links among them, though Shelley himself may have believed that his form, mythology, imagery, and symbolism hinted broadly enough at the whole chain. And just as one major clue to the intricate structure of *Adonais* must be picked up in its Platonic motto, so too the motto from Dante's Venus canzone probably offers no casual guide to *Epipsychidion.* But, as the reader may have surmised already, the Venus complex in *Epipsychidion* can be illuminated surely by parallels with the inceptive development of the complex in *The Revolt of Islam.*

The most extraordinary aspect of the complex in these poems, and in *Adonais* later, is Shelley's multiplication of Venus references. In *The Revolt of Islam,* as we have seen, the Lucifer of the Morning Star is matched by the Vesper of the beautiful woman in the introductory canto, and Laon and Cythna also relate to these twin phases of Venus. In *Epipsychidion,* Shelley and Emily appear to duplicate this sort of gemination, and in turn relate to the ideal Venusian Being as Laon and Cythna did to a heavenly Venus. More than this, Shelley's and Emily's meteoric merger remarkably recalls the fusion of the Morning Star and the Vesperlike woman into a single "clear and mighty planet." In both poems, these various interrelationships are emphasized by synesthetic interchanges, many of which intimate that light and music of the third sphere are equivalent.

It remains to observe that in *Epipsychidion* the proposed voyage of elopement to an island Venus probably parallels the boat journeys, in both the first and last cantos of *The Revolt of Islam,* to the Temple of the Spirit. This Temple, if not Venus, is presided over by a male personification of the Morning Star and is the special heavenly destination of all the Venus figures in the poem. If the island in *Epipsychidion* thus resembles the Venusian Temple of the Spirit, Shelley has worked it much more carefully into the structure of his vision narrative. It is virtually identifiable with the Being of Shelley's youthful visions and stands in the same relationship to the pair of lovers as they stand to one another. All embody a divine light, whose principal symbolic localization is in the third sphere. Much the same may be said of the interlocking Venus symbolism of *The Revolt of Islam.* The special achievement of *Epipsychidion* is the detailed, sustained, extremely refined fashion in which Venus symbolism and synesthesia cooperate within the comprehensive scheme of the embodied ray. Together, as well as in ways proper to each, they insist subtly and repeatedly that all rays, though refracted in every sort of human, natural, and celestial prism, converge in one unbroken light.

5

ADONAIS: THE ONE ASTER

I

THE synesthetic scheme of *Adonais* has marked similarities to those of *Epipsychidion* and *The Triumph of Life*. The chief resemblance lies in Shelley's further use of synesthesia as an element of the Venus complex, to which *Adonais* makes an outstanding, and certainly the best understood, contribution. The focus of the elegy's synesthesia is once more the stellar Venus and its spheral music; but along with this we have to recognize also, as extraordinarily important for the whole poem, that the star of Venus, partly by virtue of the Greek-English pun on "aster," must be thought of as a "flower of heaven." Light, music, and odor of this flower-star or aster unite synesthetically, and it is quite necessary to grasp that their union anticipates and confirms Shelley's famous celebration of the "One" in the concluding philosophical stanzas. But this is only the primary aspect of the aster scheme. A complementary pattern of "feeding" imagery also helps to bring out relationships between heavenly and earthly Venuses. The whole scheme constitutes one of Shelley's most ambitious and consistent efforts to press synesthesia into the service of his metaphysical visionary themes.

From his concern to coordinate this synesthetic scheme with certain broad patterns of imagery and symbolism, I suspect Shelley hoped that even contemporary readers of his more or less "public" tribute to Keats would guess what he was aiming at. The hope seems to have been quite vain. Indeed, not until our own time have some of the larger structural aspects of the elegy been placed in clear view. These have to do mainly with the role of Venus, and it is imperative to discuss them at some length before examining the aster scheme, which they subsume.

Yeats's magnificent pages on Shelley's Venus symbolism oddly make no mention of *Adonais.* And ironically, too, for if those pages have not been properly appreciated, there has since emerged no better understanding of Venus symbolism than in *Adonais* itself. For this we are indebted principally to Hungerford and Baker.[1] Unfortunately, no one can acknowledge this debt now without taking into account Wasserman's endeavor to annul part of it, for in an important recent essay he has chosen to revise and restrict radically their interpretation of Venus as presiding genius of the poem.[2]

Hungerford first showed how thoroughly Shelley adapted the Venus-Adonis myth in the first two-thirds of *Adonais.* This part, everyone agrees today, is not only an intricate and oblique yet essentially faithful "exercise" in the conventions of pastoral elegy. By using the myth it honors a tradition of this form reaching back to Bion's *Lament for Adonis.* Among Shelley's variants are his provocative substitution of the name Adonais for Adonis, the even more provocative alteration of Venus to "Urania," and the change of her role from that of lover to mother. These and other changes do not obscure Shelley's basic acceptance of the myth's elegiac heritage, and we have only to thank Hungerford for demonstrating how wholehearted, though perhaps extravagantly subtle, Shelley's adaptation was. But Hungerford went further, arguing that if the last third of the poem seems abruptly to reject all trace of pastoral conventions, it does not abandon the myth but sustains it on several levels, most notably a philosophical one.[3] The crux of this is that the obviously pastoral part has no analogue for the traditional consolation, which tells how dead Adonis reunites with his goddess. But since the philosophical conclusion proclaims that Adonais has returned to the One, Hungerford deduced that Shelley had here accommodated the reunion by elevating Venus-Urania to an abstract level. Accordingly, we should see that Venus-Urania, although apparently subject to mortal limitations in the pastoral part, has been revealed by the conclusion in her true character as "the Divine Love, the Platonic One," and that Adonais has immortally reunited with her "unchanging essence." [4]

For such symbolic transformation of the myth, which Hungerford deprecated as excessively ingenious,[5] Shelley may have found some precedent in Spenser.[6] It undeniably has precedents in Shelley's own verse, as Baker asserted in accepting Hungerford's thesis.[7] But its best support lies in Baker's added evidence that Venus symbolism extends throughout the poem. He demonstrated that the Platonic epigram prefixed to *Adonais* is no mere ornament (some editors go on hacking it away), but an invaluable clue to the star-of-Venus symbolism that informs the entire elegy.[8]

Addressed to "Aster," this epigram reads as follows in Shelley's own translation:

> Thou wert the morning star among the living,
> Ere thy fair light had fled;—
> Now, having died, thou art as Hesperus, giving
> New splendour to the dead.[9]

As Baker shows, the elegy requires us to see that Adonais also is an "Aster," and, like Plato's Aster, a Venus—morning star or Lucifer in life, in death evening star or Vesper (Hesperus). This need not be dwelt on here. Though Baker's reasons for Shelley's choice of this symbolism and his demonstration of its structural contribution to *Adonais* are hard to pass over, I prefer now to stress how tellingly, if curiously, the star symbolism relates to the mythical narrative. In mythical terms, Keats is an Adonis who will ultimately unite with the "unchanging essence" of Venus-Urania, so becoming an aspect of divine influence, part of "the white radiance of Eternity." But in terms of the star symbolism, Keats is from the start a Venus (Lucifer) himself; that is, as Uranian poet in life he always bears his part in mirroring divine light. Hence we can infer that the Lucifer-Vesper symbolism anticipates and implies throughout the pastoral section that mythic transformation which Hungerford discovered in the philosophical conclusion: Adonais is at all times a Venus essentially at one with Venus-Urania. I emphasize this relationship between myth and star symbolism (which reveals once again how Shelley liked to multiply Venus references), because Baker barely hints at it, and because Wasserman's failure to take the hint was disastrous for his whole approach to the elegy.

Now what were Wasserman's reservations about all this?

To begin with, he generously acknowledged a heavy obligation to Baker and in fact followed his interpretation in many basic points.[10] His one greatly consequential departure from Baker concerns the nature of Urania, whom he wished to eject altogether from the philosophical conclusion and whose significance in the pastoral section he wanted to restrict severely. Referring to Shelley scholarship in general, he argued that "a fixed set of assumptions concerning" Urania had hindered correct reading of the poem.[11] These assumptions are: in any Shelley poem a goddess named Urania must descend from Plato's Uranian Aphrodite and so be a truly spiritual ideal; in *Adonais* Urania clearly resembles Adonis's lover and so must be a Venus-Urania; and Urania, as a spiritual ideal, is probably the One of the conclusion.[12] But, Wasserman contended, while a Urania everywhere else in Shelley would pass for Platonic ideal, in the pastoral section Urania is unique: she is merely an earth-goddess, "the spirit of organic life." [13] As for the conclusion, there "Urania disappears from the poem . . . because . . . she has no relevance to the theme of spiritual immortality." [14] Urania cannot have any part in the conclusion, he insisted, because "she is opposed to, not identified with, the One, which is an Eternity outside time, an Eternity that 'remains.'" [15] Hence Adonais, in his immortal essence as a Vesper, is the very opposite of this earthly spirit, his mother. Finally, this must be the case, Wasserman said, because if we adhere to previous scholars' "externally imposed" belief "that Urania is another absolute Ideal, the One," we must confront "insurmountable difficulties . . . inside the poem." [16]

But Wasserman is badly confused and inconsistent in this. Consider why Shelley chose the name Urania for a Venus who cannot be Uranian. Following Wasserman,

Milton Wilson has charged this to "Shelley's carelessness" and hoped that "future critics" would avoid "falling into the trap." [17] If a trap, it is one of the most ingenious that care or carelessness ever fashioned. Let us pass over the grand setting of this trap in Shelley's Uranian *oeuvre* and examine its central device as Wasserman revealed it in *Adonais*. Two passages of his essay focus on it. They deal with Urania as the Venus of both Shelley's version of the myth and his star symbolism, and with the significance of Venus's star in its Lucifer-Vesper duality. (This will be especially rough going if the reader does not keep firmly in mind that Wasserman was proving, *not* the identity of Urania and Adonais, but their opposition. Two pointers may help: first, he did *not* mean to equate Urania's "astronomical role" with Adonais's; second, he *did*, incredibly, depend on "external" references to Shelley's Uranian symbolism.)

(i)

> In her astronomical role Urania, here the mother of Adonais, is the planet Venus; and in one appearance this planet is called Vesper (the evening star), in another, Lucifer (the morning star). Hence it is within the potential relations of the myth that Adonis-Adonais eventually became one manifestation of the star of Venus Urania: "thou Vesper of our throng." . . . That Shelley intended the metempsychosis from Keats-Adonais to Vesper to be central to the poem is evident in his having prefaced to it [the "Aster" epigraph].[18]

(ii)

> But by the translation of Adonais' spirit into Vesper, the poet is not asserting that death is the moment of

> soul-making. Instead, he is identifying the earthly soul with the eternal spirituality beyond the world of decay and mutability; for Vesper not only is the star of Venus (just as the mythical Adonis is related to the mythical Venus), but is also identical with Lucifer, the morning star—the point that the epigraph from Plato drives home. Lucifer-Vesper, which repeatedly serves in Shelley's poems as variant interpretations of the ideal—Love, Freedom, Good, Truth [Wasserman's note here refers to *The Revolt of Islam,* Canto I; *Hellas;* and *The Triumph of Life*]—is, therefore, the symbol of the eternal spirit, since it is always present. Were the atmosphere of mortality removed, man would perceive that the "One remains" and that "Heaven's light forever shines"; that day and night are one, life and death, Lucifer and Vesper, the spirit of the living Adonais and that of the dead. What is being asserted is that the ultimate reality of both earthly life and the post-mortal eternity is the Spiritual One.[19]

Wasserman did not realize how cunning this trap is. He warned us against Shelley's usual view of an ideal Venus and said that the Hungerford-Baker interpretation of Venus-Urania as such an ideal was "externally imposed." But in these two passages he actually showed that in *Adonais* itself Shelley himself provided them with this whole erroneous interpretation, only applying it all through the elegy to one star of Venus—the son Adonais—but nowhere to the other star of Venus, his mother. Adonais is Lucifer-Vesper, the ideal of Shelley's other verse (that is, the Venus-Urania which other scholars have mistaken Urania for). Urania is also Lucifer-Vesper but cannot be that ideal Uranian Venus. If Wasserman was correct, this *is* carelessness, and it is small wonder that others have fallen into Shelley's trap.

But why cannot Urania be the ideal or the One? If we take her as that, what are the "insurmountable difficulties" that must be faced? Outstanding among them is Urania's lament in the pastoral section:

I would give
All that I am to be as thou now art!
But I am chained to Time, and cannot thence depart!
(26, 7–9)[20]

In Wasserman's view this indicates Urania's absolute sundering from the immortal Adonais and the eternal One he joins.[21] *They* can have no connection with the temporal, material world which enchains her. To support this he quoted two passages, supposedly designed to contrast Urania and the One.[22] In the first (stanza 24) we see an apparent influence of Urania on the Many, which "Rent the soft Form they never could repel." In the second we see the supposedly contrasting influence of the One:

the one Spirit's plastic stress
Sweeps through the dull dense world, compelling there,
All new successions to the forms they wear;
Torturing th' unwilling dross that checks its flight
To its own likeness, as each mass may bear.
(43, 3–7)

But what could reveal more clearly than this second passage that the Spirit of the One is *not* "an Eternity outside time"? Wasserman, by the way, significantly omitted the immediately preceding lines, which say that the immortal Adonais "is a portion of the loveliness/ Which once he made more lovely." Obviously, both the One and Adonais, like Urania, are somehow "chained to Time," and Wasserman's two passages prove the similarity between Urania and the One, not their difference. Urania's lament is only a dramatic and ironic means of giving her grief full play and preparing for the consolatory assurance that she and Adonais are not really separated. It is indeed simply one of the many conventions of the form that Shelley accepted.

Another "insurmountable" difficulty is Shelley's making Urania the mother rather than the lover of Adonais. Arguing that she can be only an earth-bound Venus Genetrix and in no way a Platonic Venus-Urania, Wasserman wrote: "Indeed, Shelley has been rather helpfully explicit about her nature. She must be the mother of Adonais instead of his lover, just as she is also the mother of Milton, because she is *the* 'mighty Mother' [of earthly things only]." [23] But Shelley is far from being explicit in the way that Wasserman says. Milton is certainly "the third among the sons of light" [24] (Homer and Dante are usually supposed to be his two elder brothers), a son of Urania. But, surely, unless this is another cunning trap, Shelley's celebration of Milton as Urania's son must send us to the invocation of *Paradise Lost,* Book VII, where Urania's *heavenly* nature is famously displayed and Milton implicitly compares himself as her son to Orpheus as Calliope's. In *Adonais* itself the only thing earthly about Milton's being a son of light is that, like other immortal stars, he "reigns o'er earth," just as Adonais-Vesper does in the conclusion. Because of this plain similarity between Milton in the pastoral section and Adonais in the conclusion, Wasserman's contention forced him into tortured reasoning about degrees of immortality possessed by the various stars of poetry.[25] It is simpler and more satisfactory to see all poets as portions of the one light, sons of Venus Genetrix Stellarum. This harmonizes better with Shelley's thought in *A Defence of Poetry*, where he speaks of "that great poem, which all poets, like the cooperating thoughts of one great mind, have built up since the beginning of the world."[26] Venus-Urania is in effect that "one great mind." And she is mother, not lover, because her sons, like her, are Venuses, too.

I have had to deal at length with the Hungerford-Baker interpretation of Urania and with Wasserman's disagreement because a proper understanding of synesthesia in *Adonais* depends utterly on grasping its Venus symbolism. Two points seem to me basic: the first is that Venus-Urania is the One; the other is that the manifestations of Venus are multiple. Venus is therefore Many as well as One, but a qualified Many—a Many that by its nature points to or reflects the One. Thus Lucifer and Vesper are of course phases of the one Venus. Thus Adonais is also a form of Venus. Thus, too, Shelley himself, at the end of the elegy, is still another form of Venus, imagining himself about to embark on the same extraordinary starward sail that so many Venuslike spirits in his poetry take. That Venus is both One and Many, the "one great mind" of which all poets are aspects, seems to me in short the whole point in *Adonais* and elsewhere of Shelley's multiplication of Venus references. The same relationship between unity and multiplicity explains the elegy's synesthesia. Steady awareness of this must add to our realization that *Adonais*, despite some of Shelley's broad hints and despite the abundantly helpful evidence of his other work, has turned out to be an extremely complicated test of one's ability to perceive Venusian unity in variety.

II

The first synesthetic expression of *Adonais* occurs in the second stanza and weaves together images and symbols that dominate the entire poem. It establishes a pattern that is later repeated with some variation and with no simple, fixed relationship to the over-all argument that the elegy carries forward. The pattern has three easily identifiable aspects or motifs, which must be considered primary. These motifs, which I shall call stellar, musical, and floral, apply mainly to Adonais (Keats) or his poetry, but are best regarded as generally Venusian. Their application to Adonais emerges, somewhat obliquely, in the opening stanza. There we learn by implication that Adonais is a *flower*, seemingly bound by the frost of death (3), but we learn also that he will survive eternally, through "his fate and fame," as an *echo* and as a *light* (8–9). Allusion to Adonais as a flower links him with the mythical Adonis, metamorphosed at death into an anemone, and therefore hints at the start that he has not really or entirely perished, and will not be forever frost-bound. If we do not immediately suppose him an Aster, flower but also star, as the Platonic epigraph suggests and as we soon see clearly enough, this floral reference points only to the motif's mythical source. The identification of Adonais with light and echo introduces the stellar and musical motifs and indicates the other source of the pattern in star symbolism. That Adonais is a light-bearing Venus, a Lucifer, all will agree. But some may question whether the echo reference, even though Adonais's poetry has been and will continue to be what Shelley elsewhere calls an "echo of the eternal music," [27] can or need be connected with the star symbolism. Later, synesthetic combinations of Venusian music with Venusian light should make plain, however, that Adonais's poetry must be understood as an echo of planetary music, or a melody of light. Without further comment at this point on relationships among the three motifs and the myth and the star symbolism, let us see how Shelley synesthetically weaves the pattern in the second stanza.

This stanza shifts attention to Urania by expressing the traditional mourner's lament that the muse or guardian of the deceased has neglected her charge. When Adonais died, Urania appears to have been withdrawn "in her Paradise," attended by "listening Echoes." At the moment of death, or shortly thereafter, however, one of her Echoes revives the music of Adonais:

> one, with soft enamoured breath,
> Rekindled all the fading melodies,
> With which, like flowers that mock the corse beneath,
> He had adorned and hid the coming bulk of Death. (6–9)

Line seven ("Rekindled all the fading melodies") combines the three motifs of the star-music-flower pattern with remarkable succinctness. The "melodies" are expressly likened to flowers in the next line; hence the punning adjective "fading" anticipates the comparison. But these flowerlike melodies are "rekindled," as though they were dying embers or sparks. In *A Defence of Poetry,* Shelley wrote that Dante's "very words are instinct with spirit; each is as a spark, a burning atom of inextinguishable thought." [28] (The essay also refers to Dante as a Lucifer, incidentally.)[29] Presumably, Adonais's melodies are similarly burning atoms, which can be rekindled by breath, and which as fiery light represent the stellar motif of the three-part pattern. Of this complex expression it is pertinent to note also that both human breathing and plant oxidation may be thought forms of burning, both being thus referred to in a passage of *The Triumph of Life*, where we learn that flowers

> Burned slow and inconsumably, and sent
> Their odorous sighs up to the smiling air.
> (13–14)

Hence if the melodies are like flowers, these in turn, with their burning light, are like stars of earth—in short, are asters. The intricate, highly compressed metaphor of "Rekindled all the fading melodies" fuses, therefore, the stellar, floral, and musical motifs presented separately in the first stanza.

Several points about this synesthetic fusion need emphasis. It is hardly surprising that the motifs apply to Adonais in the first stanza, and then to his poetry in the second, both being essentially Venusian. But this dual application takes on great significance if we attend to the Echo's role. She truly "echoes" Adonais's poetry, having power to reproduce or "rekindle" its unusual qualities. Now, once we have grasped that the poetry itself is Venusian, part of the one "great poem" (as the *Defence* puts it), this is just what we should expect, for the Echo, as attendant on Venus-Urania, can give back *her* music as well as Adonais's. The Echo is simply an aspect of Urania on the one hand, and of Adonais on the other. Through her agency, therefore, Adonais's basic oneness with Urania already appears, even though Urania "in her Paradise" seems to have lost him. Hence, too, from Urania's perspective we see that his poetry echoes her planetary music.

Synesthetically, in the interwoven motifs, his poetry has similar implications. Urania, as I have argued, is both One and Many. To the various multiplications of Venus references already noted, we can now add evidence that Adonais's poetry ("melodies") duplicates Venus's music. But what could be fitter than that this music by itself should reveal unity in multiplicity? In poem after poem Shelley has been telling us that music and light of the third sphere are equivalent and that the melody of light is in effect a single emanation, capable of affecting all the senses. Here, in the second stanza of *Adonais*, the synesthetic equivalence of light or fire, odor, and music suggests that they participate in an ultimate unity, and this revelation of unity in multiplicity must, I take it, essentially characterize Adonais's poetry. Hence his poetry must echo Venus's music in the special sense that it, too, is a complex melody of light. Hence, also, the star-music-flower motifs are doubly Venusian: each motif, taken separately, relates somehow to Venus; and their synesthetic union underscores the Venusian theme of One and Many.

So far as concerns the three motifs, Shelley's method of first presenting them separately, as in the first stanza, and then interweaving them, as in the second, continues on various scales and with various refinements throughout the rest of the poem. In stanzas 4 and 5, Keats's poetic predecessors are described as stars (Milton alone being clearly alluded to). We may guess that all, like Adonais, have been Lucifers, though not equally brilliant. The author calls on Urania, as one who has lamented the fate of all these "sons of light," to weep now for her latest loss. In stanza 6, this version of the stellar motif is dropped, Adonais being described throughout in floral terms. He is lightly alluded to as a flower in stanza 7 and then clearly so described again in stanza 10. Meanwhile, in stanzas 3 and 9, we note the musical motif in complaints that Adonais's voice is now muted, his music no longer echoed on earth. In these versions of the motifs, one may detect slight hints of their interrelationships, but these seem too faint for profitable notice here. In stanza 11, however, quite broad hints appear, as personified survivals of Adonais's music (for it does survive, despite all the surface statements to the contrary) minister to his corpse with "starry dew," throw wreaths of clipped hair upon it, and otherwise signal an interweaving of the motifs. But they are not plainly interwoven until stanza 12.

This tells how a still vital "Splendour" of Adonais's poetry attempts to renew its strength at the dead poet's lips:

> Another Splendour on his mouth alit,
> That mouth, whence it was wont to draw the breath
> Which gave it strength to pierce the guarded wit,
> And pass into the panting heart beneath
> With lightning and with music: the damp death
> Quenched its caress upon his icy lips;
> And, as a dying meteor stains a wreath
> Of moonlight vapour, which the cold night clips,
> It flushed through his pale limbs, and passed to its eclipse.

Here we can see a number of parallels with the interweaving of the motifs in the second stanza. There an Echo's breath rekindled Adonais's melodies. Now a Splendour seeks to have its "lightning," which is also "music," rekindled by the breath of Adonais. Thus Shelley interweaves two of the motifs in virtually the same fashion as before. To complete the scheme he must suggest that Adonais's breath is like the "breath" or "burning" of a flower. This he does unmistakably, though perhaps with some strain: the Splendour flushing through Adonais's limbs is likened to a "meteor" momentarily illuminating a "wreath" of vapor; Adonais by implication is wreathlike or flowerlike. And since the "flush" of life with which the Splendour endows the corpse is meteoric, we are reminded that Adonais is starlike also. All this indicates, therefore, that Adonais's breath is or has been a single medium for fiery light, music, and odor, and that he himself must be conceived of not only as poet and source of music, but also as flower-star or aster.

The first interweaving of the motifs related specially to an Echo; the second to a Splendour. As we might expect, the next, which occurs in stanza 20, gives prominence to the third, floral motif. Before this, Shelley once again treats the motifs separately, associating them with a series of lamenting personifications—Morning, the Echo of classical myth, and Spring, probably intended to be a kind of classical Flora. In stanza 14, Morning so laments that she hides "the aëreal eyes that kindle day." This, in my opinion, weakly introduces the stellar motif, but suffices by pointing to an obscuring of heavenly lights. Stanza 15 is devoted entirely to Echo, unable now to "mimic" any sounds at all, because she is wholly preoccupied with grief over Adonais's "remembered lay." Shelley plays synesthetically on her legendary metamorphosis, while telling us that Adonais means more to her than Narcissus:

> she can mimic not his lips, more dear
> Than those for whose disdain she pined away
> Into a shadow of all sounds. (6–8)

Then, in stanza 16, we learn that the grieving Spring has thrown down her "buds" as autumn throws down leaves.

Shelley makes it plain that "her delight," Adonais, has been this Flora's prime flower of all by referring to Hyacinthus and Narcissus as his lamenting "companions."

All three personifications—Morning, Echo, Spring—act "unnaturally," as though they were Night, Silence, Autumn. And it is their very grief which is made to appear unnatural, because through it they pervert or leave off their ordinary functions. Somewhat cryptically, Shelley is saying that to grieve for Adonais is wrong because he has not really perished; it is their grief that is their loss, not their loss that is their grief. I do not want to expatiate on this, but had to touch on it, for the next interweaving of the motifs is a particularly cryptic rejoinder to the surface despair of the text. Shelley prepares for it, after the separate treatments of the motifs just noted, by dwelling (in stanzas 18ff.) on the mixed joy and bitterness that must mark the return of spring without Adonais. In all this, of course, he employs the traditional contrast between natural and human life, the one being forever renewed after its death each year, the other never.

Stanza 20 macabrely heightens this contrast. Shelley has described (stanza 19) the spirit of "quickening life" that bursts forth every spring. Now he writes:

> The leprous corpse, touched by this spirit tender,
> Exhales itself in flowers of gentle breath;
> Like incarnations of the stars, when splendour
> Is changed to fragrance, they illumine death
> And mock the merry worm that wakes beneath.
> (1–5)

This third interweaving of the motifs recalls both of the earlier ones, but especially that in stanza 2. In all three, "breath" is stressed as the medium of light, odor, and music. Here, admittedly, music must be understood in "mock," which is ambiguous. This reading is greatly helped, however, by recalling that the melodies in stanza 2 were compared to mocking flowers. Here it is particularly notable how Shelley insists that the flowers' splendor and fragrance are one in their burning breath. He first asks us only, in effect, to add to the age-old flower-star comparison the fact that each has its own emanation, odor in the one case, light in the other. Then his unexpected use of "illumine" requires us to imagine that the flowers' odor *is* light. This, too, by showing that the flowers are truly asters, encourages the supposition that their light and odor must also be musical.

The phrase "incarnations of the stars" gives the most nearly overt verbal evidence in the poem for the assumption I have made all along—that in the "Aster" of the Platonic epigraph Shelley wishes us to recognize a pun. This has many bearings on the imagery and symbolism of the elegy, a number of which have already been mentioned or implied, such as that Adonais, the Lucifer and Vesper of the epigraph, is really an aster, both star *and* flower. Basically, however, all of these bearings converge in the single one that every aster of the poem is Venusian and belongs to a multiple unity. The above passage, taken in context, insists on the surface that the flowers contrast with Adonais, enjoying a general rebirth that excludes him; more than this, they revive at his expense, spring from his corpse. But these flowers, as asters, are so many Venuses, sharing the relationship to Venus-Urania that Adonais himself has. In this sense, they are not opposite to him but identical. Interweaving of the three motifs here particularly invites us to link the flowers with Adonais's poetry by revealing that they have the same synesthetic, Venusian qualities that the

"Echo" and the "Splendour" of his poetry had. And through this we can again anticipate the consolatory argument of the elegy's conclusion: "He is made one with Nature" (stanza 42, line 1).

This part of the poem closes in stanza 21 with seemingly desperate comment on human subjection to time. The eight stanzas that follow (22–29) tell how Urania, finally aroused to Adonais's plight, speeds to his death chamber, attempts to revive him, and then laments her failure and her loss. These stanzas contain many parallels with earlier passages and carry along the three-part pattern of the star-music-flower motifs: Urania has marked affinities (1) with the spirit of "quickening life" which produces flowers; (2) with the "Splendour" of Adonais's poetry, she herself being called a "Splendour" in stanza 22; and (3) with the classical Echo. Similarly: (1) on her way to Adonais, Urania suffers injury from human spirits' rough resistance to this "soft" but irresistible "Form," and her "sacred blood" leaves behind a trail of "eternal flowers" (stanza 24); (2) she repeats, in stanza 25, the action of the "Splendour" that returned to Adonais's lips; through her "might," the corpse blushes, breath revisits the lips, and "Life's pale light" flashes through the limbs; (3) and next, in stanza 26, she is much like Echo, begging Adonais for one more word, as well as one more kiss, to cherish in memory. Hence all the motifs are now directly associated with Urania, their ultimate Venusian source. Though only in stanza 25 is there anything like an attempt to unite them again synesthetically, we cannot now be unmindful of their Venusian unity and all that this implies. Nor can Urania's grief, even while it recalls and seems to surpass the grief of the deluded Morning, Echo, and Spring, cloud entirely her awareness that Adonais is immortal. Though she laments that his life was cut off too soon, before his spirit "filled its crescent sphere" (stanza 27), she knows that the "immortal stars awake again" in "the spirit's awful night" (stanza 29). Even in the depth of grief, therefore, she is asserting that Adonais-Lucifer may be eclipsed but must reappear as Adonais-Vesper. Nevertheless, despite this hint and the echo of the three-part pattern, the superficial emphasis of the elegy at this point is on Adonais's eclipse.

The eclipse approaches totality in stanzas 30–35, and the darkening of Venusian light is accompanied by an appropriate variation of the three-part pattern. Urania having ceased her lament, these stanzas bring in a procession of mourning poets: Byron, Thomas Moore, Shelley himself, and Leigh Hunt. The three-part pattern, designedly faint and diffuse, appears in the subtly dramatized autobiographical stanzas, 31–34, which no one can read aright, in my opinion, without seeing that the Shelley in the poem must be related to both Adonais and Urania—that he is himself a Venus, but an aster temporarily gone "astray." He is "a dying lamp" rather than a star; if a flower, he is "withering"; if a singer, he remains unheard because his are "accents of an unknown land." Everything about him suggests a pale reflection of the Adonais in whose fate he now weeps his own, a phantom "Form" beside the "Form" of Urania. "A Love in desolation masked," he is so unworthy a Venus that, while Byron and the others recognize a fellow, only "of less note," Urania takes him for a stranger and must ask, "Who art thou?" In short, this Shelley suffers in life the eclipse that he imagines for the dead Adonais. And he, as a dark aster, most fitly pronounces the curse against the supposed murderer of Adonais, which—in stanzas 36–37—brings us to the extreme darkness of bitter grief; though strictly, perhaps, these stanzas belong to the author of the elegy, as distinguished from his dramatic projection.

III

Stanza 38 marks the famous "turning point" of the poem, beginning the philosophical conclusion. While still addressing Keats's "murderer" in this stanza, the author now proclaims that the spirit of Adonais has returned "to the burning fountain whence it came." Here and throughout the rest of the elegy, Adonais is either directly described or variously symbolized as a heavenly star in order, now that he is clearly proclaimed a "portion of the Eternal," to emphasize that aspcct of his asterhood. In this stanza, for example, Shelley comes closer than ever before in the poem to telling us outright that Adonais is Venus: to the murderer he says, "Thou canst not soar where he is sitting now," thus clearly echoing a boast of Milton's Satan (*Paradise Lost*, IV, 829), who was to Shelley, we know, a true though somewhat lackluster *Lucifer*. (Not until stanza 46 is Adonais plainly called "Vesper.") Eclipse now ends for Urania, too. From this point on, as I have argued in support of Hungerford and Baker, she disappears from the poem as an anthropomorphic muse or goddess and becomes instead the "One" of "the white radiance of Eternity." In keeping with these transformations are certain changes in the way Shelley resumes his interweaving of the three-part pattern. His synesthetic practice in the conclusion does not differ radically from what has gone before. Metaphorically, however, it is much less rich and striking, at least so far as concerns fusions of the three motifs—presumably because

Shelley now, with a perspective generally opposite to that which prevailed earlier, wishes to stress supernal unity and permanence at the expense of earthly variety and change. And this practice sometimes becomes taxingly oblique.

The conclusion most clearly renews the primary pattern of the first two-thirds in stanza 49, which falls within a passage telling the proper attitude to take toward the immortal Adonais:

> Go thou to Rome,—at once the Paradise,
> The grave, the city, and the wilderness;
> And where its wrecks like shattered mountains rise,
> And flowering weeds, and fragrant copses dress
> The bones of Desolation's nakedness
> Pass, till the spirit of the spot shall lead
> Thy footsteps to a slope of green access
> Where, like an infant's smile, over the dead
> A light of laughing flowers along the grass is spread.

The last two lines here directly echo the synesthetic interweavings of the three motifs in stanza 2 (where melodies are like flowers that mock a buried corpse) and stanza 20 (where starlike flowers mock the grave worm). In Keats's Roman burial ground, the mockery of laughing, radiant flowers is once again a music of asters, directed most notably now against all misguided, mortal lamenting for the dead-living Adonais. This synesthetic passage, like those in the earlier stanzas, follows separate presentations of the three motifs. In stanza 49 itself, the flower motif is apparent enough in the "flowering weeds" that deck the nineteenth-century Rome. Three previous stanzas, 44–46, describe a heaven of poet-stars which now, along with Chatterton, Sidney, and Lucan, includes Adonais as its Vesper. It is also, of course, a "Heaven of Song." But Shelley may have wanted us to recognize the motif of music likewise, or even particularly, in the mourner, introduced in stanza 47, who must recall the Uranian Echo (stanza 2) and other seemingly ineffectual or misguided mourners of the first two-thirds of the elegy (the Splendor of stanza 12, the classical Echo of stanza 15, Urania herself).

This unmistakable variation of the three-part pattern—the whole running from stanza 44 through 51—helps us to perceive in the conclusion other, rather difficult, treatments of this primary scheme. The first, preceding the passage just discussed, barely sketches the usual separate presentation of the motifs. This occurs in stanza 41, which harks back to the laments of Morning, Echo, and Spring (stanzas 14–16), and states or implies that their respective splendor, music, and flowery beauty have been restored now that Adonais is truly known. His spirit, indeed, *is* their splendor, music, and loveliness, as we learn immediately:

He is made one with Nature: there is heard
His voice in all her music, from the moan
Of thunder, to the song of night's sweet bird;
He is a presence to be felt and known
In darkness and in light, from herb and stone,
Spreading itself where'er that Power may move
Which has withdrawn his being to its own;
Which wields the world with never-wearied love,
Sustains it from beneath, and kindles it above.

He is a portion of the loveliness
Which once he made more lovely: he doth bear
His part, while the one Spirit's plastic stress
Sweeps through the dull dense world, compelling there,
All new successions to the forms they wear;
Torturing th' unwilling dross that checks its flight

To its own likeness, as each mass may bear;
And bursting in its beauty and its might
From trees and beasts and men into the Heaven's light.
(stanzas 42–43)

The imagery here is not synesthetic, and we must ask what this means, since previous separate presentations of the three motifs have been followed by synesthetic fusions —in stanzas 2, 12, and 20—and after the above passage the same pattern completes itself again in stanza 49. In the present instance Shelley's practice will be best understood if we first note how it relates Adonais to Venus-Urania. This passage should recall stanzas 22–29, which present Venus-Urania as Flora, Splendor, and Echo, and so associate her with all the motifs while making little or no attempt to underscore this association by means of synesthetic language. In this earlier passage we need only recognize in Venus-Urania the ultimate source of all quickening loveliness, light, and music. In the passage now under examination, Adonais clearly resembles her as such. The parallel, in short, helps to demonstrate what, according to Hungerford and Baker, this passage itself asserts so plainly, that Adonais is one with the "Power" that is Venus-Urania. (My approach to these two passages thus offers further reason for rejecting Wasserman's attempt to disjoin the immortal Adonais from Urania.) Hence, as with Venus-Urania earlier, so now with an Adonais participant in the "one Spirit," Shelley omits the usual interweaving of the motifs. But on this occasion he makes explicit what then had to be inferred about relationships between the One and the Many. Instead of simply providing hints, either in synesthetic imagery or in association of the motifs with a Venus figure, he states the intellectual basis for his whole synesthetic scheme. And distinctly now, we should see, he emphasizes and exalts unity at the expense of multiplicity, "th' unwilling dross" being compelled toward likeness to the One.

The other difficult treatment of the primary scheme follows a famous passage which once again exalts unity: "The One remains, the many change and pass . . ." (stanza 52). The three motifs here have a primarily autobiographical application and recall how the author depicted himself among the procession of mourning poets (stanzas 31–34). The first of the three, it is true, refers to the Roman environment, but the author, having directed a mourner to Keats's grave, goes along in imagination and makes the scene definitely his own. He says:

> Rome's azure sky,
> Flowers, ruins, statues, music, words are weak
> The glory they transfuse with fitting truth to speak.
> (52, 7–9)

The "speaking" here, itself weakly synesthetic, must be taken in context as an *echo* of the "glory" of the One. The other two motifs appear in the next stanza as the author complains that his earthly "hopes are gone" and that "*light* is passed from the revolving year" (emphasis added), and then compares himself to a *flower*, about to "wither" in this unstable life. In all this, the pattern is designedly faint and oblique, as before in the earlier autobiographical stanzas, where the author appeared as a dim reflection of Venus and Adonais—"a dying lamp," a "withering flower," a voice "unknown" to Urania. Now we find him once again a humble Venus figure, a dark aster, but one hoping for an elevation in death similar to Adonais's: "Adonais calls! oh, hasten thither,/ No more let Life divide what Death can join together" (stanza 53).

After this preparation, the three-part pattern receives its final unifying treatment in stanza 54, the next-to-last of the poem:

> That Light whose smile kindles the Universe,
> That Beauty in which all things work and move,
> That Benediction which the eclipsing Curse
> Of birth can quench not, that sustaining Love
> Which through the web of being blindly wove
> By man and beast and earth and air and sea,
> Burns bright or dim, as each are mirrors of
> The fire for which all thirst; now beams on me
> Consuming the last clouds of cold mortality.

Although this is extremely complex (in itself, in its relationship to the elegy as a whole, and in its multiple allusions to Dante's *Paradiso*),[30] clearly the "sustaining Love" here is Venus-Urania, celebrated chiefly as light and fire. She is the sum of Light, Beauty, and Benediction; and the first and third of these, thus associated with her and one another, show convincingly once again an interweaving or fusion of the motifs. The role of the kindling *Light* is obvious. The Benediction is a "speaking" that contrasts with the "speaking" just noted in stanza 52: the latter weakly *echoes* the One's glory; the Benediction, uneclipsed and unquenched, is itself, by virtue of the synesthetic metaphors, a burning glory, and so equivalent to the kindling Light. Hence both Light and Benediction are one with the Love that "Burns bright or dim." In view of all this, we cannot doubt how to take the "Beauty" of the triad: it must be the starry beauty that, throughout the elegy as well as in this stanza, is reflected in all "flowers" which are also asters, "mirrors" of Love's light and fire—*specula Veneris.*

But since these mirrors "thirst" for love, Shelley's metaphorical boldness compels us now, as never before in the poem, to take account of a synesthetic complication of the flower-star-music scheme. Lines 4–8 of this stanza undoubtedly owe much to *Paradiso,* XXIX, 136–145, and Shelley's "feeding" metaphor here may have been immediately influenced by one line of Cary's translation: "The fountain at whose source these drink their beams";[31] but feeding images and concepts appear throughout *Adonais* and are disposed according to a pattern that complements the main synesthetic scheme. Before turning to consider this, I would only interject that Shelley's penultimate stanza itself sufficiently suggests to what extent my "main" and "complementary," "primary" and "secondary" are merest conveniences.

IV

Feeding imagery and symbolism in *Adonais* are broadly organized according to a basic opposition between destructive and vivifying forces. On one side stands the "eternal Hunger" of Death and Corruption (stanza 8). It has many appearances and agents, both physical and spiritual. It appears most naturally, and perhaps most grotesquely, in the worms and flowers that variously feed on Adonais's corpse (stanza 20). It takes a similar guise in metaphorical "vultures" that "feed where Desolation first has fed" and in "carrion kites" (stanzas 28, 38). An "unpastured dragon," it is allied with wolves and ravens, and with the hounds of the Actaeon myth (stanzas 27, 28, 31). More abstractly, it is the Death that "feeds on [Adonais's] mute voice," the "fear and grief [that] consume us," the "cold hopes [that] swarm like worms within our living clay," and the "slow fire" of devouring Time (stanzas 3, 39, 50). All this is clear and consistent, if on occasion somewhat Gothically strained.

Another aspect of this destructive force deserves special emphasis, because it contrasts more precisely than the above with the opposing imagery of vital feeding. It appears in one of Shelley's many adaptations from his Greek elegiac models, the "translation" in stanza 36 of four lines from Moschus's *Lament for Bion.* Shelley also used these lines as a motto for his preface to the poem, their appropriateness being obvious if one recalls how much he believed "the poisoned shaft" of criticism hastened Keats's death. In Andrew Lang's prose version they read: "Poison came, Bion, to thy mouth—thou didst know poison. To such lips as thine did it come and was not sweetened? What mortal was so cruel that could mix poison for thee, or who could give thee the venom that heard thy voice? Surely he had no music in his soul" (lines 111–114).[32] Here is Shelley's adaptation:

> Our Adonais has drunk poison—oh!
> What deaf and viperous murderer could crown
> Life's early cup with such a draught of woe?
> The nameless worm would now itself disown:
> It felt, yet could escape, the magic tone
> Whose prelude held all envy, hate, and wrong,
> But what was howling in one breast alone,
> Silent with expectation of the song. (36, 1–8)

In variously shaping the "eternal Hunger," Shelley may have wished us to understand, partly by metaphorical and symbolic hints, that destructive forces threaten to "swallow up" primarily the music, light, and flowers of Venus. But this seems doubtful, even though occasional phrasing (supported of course by much of the poem's argument) suggests it. The case is quite different, however, when we come to consider the other side of his feeding imagery and symbolism. This, in contrast to the metaphorically mixed poison of the above passage, displays itself in various forms of physical and spiritual nourishment, all deriving ultimately from "that sustaining Love"; it also displays itself in unmistakable association with the primary pattern of flowers, music (or poetry), and light and fire. The association with flowers is made most apparent by allusion in stanza 6 to Keats's *Isabella* (stanzas 52–54): Shelley likens Adonais to a "nursling" of Urania,

> who grew,
> Like a pale flower by some sad maiden cherished,
> And fed with true-love tears, instead of dew.
> (2–4)

Tears substitute repeatedly for dew elsewhere in the first two-thirds of the elegy (most plainly in stanzas 10 and 16), but always with the implication that they cannot avail against the "frost" of death, not even the "fiery tears" of Urania (stanzas 1, 2). This superficially contrasts "flowers" like Adonais with natural flowers: the former die and can never be nursed back to life by tears, their only "dew"; ordinary flowers revive each spring "with life's sacred thirst" (stanzas 19–20). Cryptically, however, we are being led to the revelation that asters survive by that "fire for which all thirst."

Music or poetry, the "potable gold" of Shelley's *Defence*,[33] is also clearly presented in terms of feeding. We learn in stanza 9 that the poetic dreams, passions, and thoughts of Adonais

> were his flocks, whom near the living streams
> Of his young spirit he fed, and whom he taught
> The love which was its music. (3–5)

A usage somewhat different from this occurs in the classical Echo's mourning for Adonais: she "feeds her grief with his remembered lay" (stanza 15). Feeding of this kind may be thought destructive rather than vivifying, especially if one examines in isolation the entire stanza devoted to Echo. Here Shelley obviously wants to refine on her legend by asserting that if grief for Narcissus caused Echo to waste away until only her voice remained, greater grief for Adonais now causes the voice to dwindle. Hence to feed her grief is to starve whatever life she has. A similar reading seems required for the passage in stanza 26 which closely parallels Urania's mourning with Echo's:

> Stay yet awhile! speak to me once again;
> Kiss me, so long but as a kiss may live;
> And in my heartless breast and burning brain
> That word, that kiss, shall all thoughts else survive,
> With food of saddest memory kept alive. (1–5)

But both this passage and the Echo stanza imply plainly enough that the voice of Adonais was a source of sustenance. Silenced, the voice would "feed" only memory or grief and so could be taken as destructive. We know, however, that Urania and Echo mislead themselves in believing that it is silenced. Hence when it is rediscovered as a voice heard "in all [Nature's] music" (stanza 42), they must again know its power to nourish.

These associations of vital feeding, first with flowers, then with music, are better indicated by definite verbal clues than its association with light and fire, or stars. For this the plainest verbal clue—aside from the highly significant one in "fire for which all thirst"—occurs in Shelley's likening Adonais to an "eagle, who . . . could scale/ Heaven, and could nourish in the sun's domain/ Her mighty youth with morning" (stanza 17). For other and better evidence of the association we must look for "feeding," not of stars, but of asters or flower-stars. (To some extent this means simply that it is now convenient to touch aspects of the aster symbolism which the discussion of flower-feeding passed over.) Ordinary flowers may be said to have the natural power, as Shelley put it in another poem, of changing light into fragrance.[34] The same power is alluded to in *Adonais* in the lines, already noted but without mention of this point, which refer to flowers as "incarnations of the stars, when splendour/ Is changed to fragrance" (stanza 20). Such "incarnations" are of course asters, as their power to "illumine" so dramatically emphasizes. Asters, in other words, feed on light and convert it to fragrance which is lightlike. (This hints at one sense in which the flowers of stanza 20 "mock"—that is, imitate—"the merry worm that wakes beneath.") What follows from all this, I believe, is that some notion of feeding, or vital conversion, probably inheres in much of Shelley's aster symbolism, especially as it relates Adonais to Venus-Urania. For example, if he as her "nursling" is a flower in stanza 6, he is at the same time, by the implication of the two preceding stanzas, her nursling as a star or one "among the sons of light."

One last point about the imagery and symbolism of vital feeding deserves mention. Almost all of the examples to show its association with the primary motifs of flowers-music-stars were drawn from the first two-thirds of the elegy. This signifies, as suggested mainly in the last paragraph, that the vital feeding helps to bring out relationships between earthly and heavenly Venuses by emphasizing division and dependence. Little of it occurs in the conclusion, which stresses union and Adonais's absorption into the One; it appears there to characterize Shelley as an earthbound aster, one of the "mirrors of/ The fire for which all thirst." Adonais himself has become part of "the burning fountain."

6

PROMETHEUS UNBOUND: WORLD HARMONY

I

As INDICATED briefly in Chapter 1, the synesthetic scheme of *Prometheus Unbound* (composed in 1818–1819) exhibits two principal aspects. One is its relationship to Venus symbolism—and with this, naturally, to all the other schemes chiefly discussed in the last three chapters. The other, leading me to entitle it the stream-of-sound, is its extraordinarily marked dependence on water figures and symbols. Both aspects of the stream-of-sound, especially as they bear on the poem's theme of world harmony, present challenging difficulties, such as justify my disregard of chronology in postponing discussion of *Prometheus Unbound* to this point. For Shelley's use of synesthesia as part of the Venus complex, there has of course been considerable preparation. But his synesthetic water imagery and symbolism have so far drawn notice only in occasional, somewhat casual occurrences in *Alastor* and *The Revolt of*

Islam, which offer quite limited insight into their systematic deployment in *Prometheus Unbound.* Here, then, is the logical place to examine *Orpheus,* for this neglected fragment, while important synesthetically in itself and deserving of treatment as such, is even more important as a guide to the complexities of the stream-of-sound.

Unfortunately, though most interestingly, *Orpheus* itself needs a word of introduction, because none of Shelley's poems has suffered a stranger editorial and critical fate than this, all owing to a stream-of-sound metaphor. A blank-verse dialogue of 124 lines, the fragment remained unpublished until 1862, when Richard Garnett, who assigned its composition to 1820, edited it for his *Relics of Shelley.*[1] But Garnett had reason to doubt that *Orpheus* was in fact one of Shelley's relics. As he says in a short preface, it survived only in a "transcript" by Mary Shelley, a circumstance which would mean little were it not for one curious entry, no part of the poem itself. This is an Italian sentence: "Aspetto fin che il diluvio cala, ed allora cerco di posare argine alle sue parole" (which Garnett translated, "I await the descent of the flood, and then I endeavour to embank his words").[2] The metaphor and its Italian dress provoked in Garnett a whole series of speculations, though he expressed only some of them in his preface; others were passed on to C. D. Locock, who recorded them in his Shelley edition of 1911 along with still other speculations of his own.[3] All their conjectures, in essence, reflect skepticism about Shelley's authorship.

Truly fascinated by the Italian sentence, these editors concocted from it a fascinating but extremely dubious story. It mainly enchanted them with the idea that Mary, acting as an "amanuensis," took down an experiment in improvisation, and that in the background, possibly the foreground, of this experiment stood the brilliant Italian improviser Tommaso Sgricci, whom the Shelleys knew in the winter of 1820–1821 as both performer and acquaintance. If *Orpheus* was really Shelley's, they thought, it must have resulted from his attempt to emulate Sgricci. But quite possibly it represented or somehow reflected a performance of Sgricci himself. Or, less excitingly, it may have been someone's translation from an Italian work. If at all scrutinized, however, these and similar conjectures have little or no plausibility, and two points about the Italian sentence expose them as superfluous, to say the least. First, the presence of Italian in Shelley manuscripts is far from uncommon and frequently evidences Shelley's efforts to translate his own poetry into that language.[4] Second, the Italian metaphor chimes perfectly with a run of similar though more complex metaphors in *Orpheus* itself. The latter point apparently escaped Garnett, though his otherwise mysterious guess about *translation* argues in his favor. It certainly escaped Locock altogether.[5] Both points "explain" the Italian sentence quite simply. The sole improvisation which need in fact pertain to the fragment is that of the subject, Orpheus himself. But even this patent classical lead seems to have been lost on Garnett and Locock, so infatuated were they by Sgricci.

Yet their suspicious detractions of *Orpheus* have virtually excised it from the Shelley canon, as a glance at such scholars and critics as Grabo, Baker, Fogle, Rogers, Bloom, Wilson, and King-Hele will confirm, for these never so much as mention it. Others, like White and Butter, allude to it only incidentally.[6] Never, in short, has it attracted serious examination as a substantial fragment of Shelley's maturity.[7] Perhaps this neglect is merited. But if the long silence over *Orpheus* means acceptance of the editorial and critical opinions of Garnett and Locock, protest is rather overdue. Surely, from what I have indicated, one is entitled to wonder about their knowledge of, as Garnett put it, "the internal evidence of the piece." [8] A fresh look at that evidence might provoke wonder about their opinions, too. Here, however, treating *Orpheus* from a limited point of view and with a special aim, I need and wish only to maintain that its use of synesthesia is so characteristically Shelleyan as to make question of its true authorship appear idle.

II

The synesthesia of the dialogue is devoted entirely to description of Orpheus's improvisations. The two speakers are a person designated only as A and a Chorus, the latter playing a distinctly minor role. In the opening speech (lines 1–34) A sets the scene in a gloomy, barren, thoroughly sinister landscape, dominated by a hill cave which sends forth a poisonous mist. In this setting, however, above the sighing of blasted cypress boughs, the Chorus hears a wonderfully melodious, if mournful, sound and asks what it can be (35–37). A identifies it as the distant, wind-borne "voice of Orpheus' lyre" (38–43). The Chorus, in the last of its two brief intrusions, then expresses questioning surprise that Orpheus continues to sing after his loss of Eurydice (43–45). In the remainder of the fragment (45–124) A, assuring the Chorus that grief had only temporarily silenced Orpheus, compares his song and music as it is now in lament with what it had been while Eurydice lived and tells of its wonder-working powers. Much of this falls into synesthetic patterns, which will recall those Shelley uses in *Alastor* and *Epipsychidion* to bring out relations between a visionary and his ideal. In this case, of course, the visionary is Orpheus, the lost ideal Eurydice.

Almost twenty lines of A's last speech describe Orpheus's song and music as a stream-of-sound. But a prelusive hint of this appears when A, on first identifying the sound of the lyre, says that the winds

> bear along with them
> The waning sound, scattering it like dew
> Upon the startled sense. (41–43)

The stream-of-sound proper I shall consider in two parts. The first describes the Orphic music before Eurydice's death and descent into Hell:

> In times long past, when fair Eurydice
> With her bright eyes sat listening by his side,
> He gently sang of high and heavenly themes.
> As in a brook, fretted with little waves
> By the light airs of spring—each riplet makes
> A many-sided mirror for the sun,
> While it flows musically through green banks,
> Ceaseless and pauseless, ever clear and fresh,
> So flowed his song, reflecting the deep joy
> And tender love that fed those sweetest notes,
> The heavenly offspring of ambrosial food.
> (56–66)

While here the sound-water analogy is basic, we should notice especially how it also functions as a medium for comparison between song and light. Eurydice must be associated with a sunlike ideal, to which the stream of music, at this point, presents a perfectly responsive mirror. Shelley succeeds in treating the whole without any sense of strain, since streams can of course be imagined readily as both musical and reflective. But "offspring" (66), if it is meant as a pun, and the feeding metaphors at the close may appear to be rather disturbingly introduced.

The second part describes how Orpheus sings after his failure to rescue Eurydice from the underworld. And again Shelley makes the stream-of-sound accommodate a comparison between song and light:

> Returning from drear Hell,
> He chose a lonely seat of unhewn stone,
> Blackened with lichens, on a herbless plain.
> Then from the deep and overflowing spring
> Of his eternal ever-moving grief
> There rose to Heaven a sound of angry song.
> 'Tis as a mighty cataract that parts
> Two sister rocks with waters swift and strong,
> And casts itself with horrid roar and din
> Adown a steep; from a perennial source
> It ever flows and falls, and breaks the air
> With loud and fierce, but most harmonious roar,
> And as it falls casts up a vaporous spray
> Which the sun clothes in hues of Iris light.
> Thus the tempestuous torrent of his grief
> Is clothed in sweetest sounds and varying words
> Of poesy. Unlike all human works,
> It never slackens. (67–84)

Now, instead of being a smooth mirror for sunlight, the stream-of-sound has become a rough, clouded torrent. But the stream is not wholly darkened. Its spray, at least, acts prismatically to let sunlight through in rainbow form. Hence when this part is compared with the previous, it appears plain that Orpheus's two states regarding Eurydice equate respectively with the two states of the stream-of-sound regarding light. While Eurydice lived, the stream resembled the pure light itself. Now that she is a shade, and merely remembered, the stream has only a rainbow fringe. Original as it is, all this so strikingly recalls Shelley's customary means of adapting synesthesia to his vision theme that comment is hardly necessary.

This stream-of-sound passage is followed by an obviously related but less impressive synesthetic description of Orpheus's lament. It is similar because A now likens the lament to a streaming wind, at first a stormy blast which darkens the evening sky, but later a clearing breeze which reveals a "serene Heaven" of stars and moon (87–97). A bit of verbal play on the words "echo" and "picture" underscores Shelley's synesthetic intention:

> I talk of moon, and wind, and stars, and not
> Of song; but, would I echo his high song,
> Nature must lend me words ne'er used before,
> Or I must borrow from her perfect works,
> To picture forth his perfect attributes.
> (98–102)

This suggests an odd refinement of *ut pictura poesis*: the Orphic song, or *poesis*, can be represented (echoed) only by *poesis* which attempts to be *pictura*. But if Shelley trifles in this fashion, we must see that basically he wants to equate the Orphic *poesis* with a world harmony (Nature's "perfect works"), or with a force working toward world harmony. This becomes manifest in the remainder of A's speech, carrying us to the end of the fragment.

A now reverts to the situation of the bereaved Orpheus in that "herbless plain" (so called in line 69 and now again in 104) which is a parallel to the wasteland of this very scene, and describes how his song converts all to an earthly paradise. Details of Orpheus's wonderful influence upon flora and fauna of the most diverse kinds are familiar enough from ancient versions of the myth. I would only stress, first, Shelley's careful contrast between this harmonious paradise of Orpheus's creation and the scene of the fragment as described in A's opening speech and, second, the implications for the latter, as a dark, poisonous wasteland, of that Orphic "dew" which A identified for the Chorus. When these points are weighed, we must infer that the stream-of-sound (fundamentally a love song, be it remembered) could potentially bring the world, as well as the "herbless plain," to fertility, radiance, and harmony. And I stress this because what is potential in the stream-of-sound of *Orpheus* becomes actual in its far more complex counterpart in *Prometheus Unbound.*

III

The descriptive movement in *Orpheus* from wasteland, through stream-of-sound, to earthly paradise suggests in miniature the plan of *Prometheus Unbound,* Acts I–III, which appears to have satisfied Shelley for some while as a work complete in itself.[9] Through most of Act I, the chained Prometheus's world, physical and moral, is wintrily desolate. Hope for its regeneration depends on his enduring power to forgive and love—love being "the liquid joy of life" (I, 766)—and toward the end of the act promising clouds and vapors, parallels to the dew of Orphic music, gather in a prelude to the stream-of-sound. In Act II, which treats mainly the experience of Prometheus's wife Asia and her sister Panthea, the stream-of-sound bears these two "Oceanides" on an extremely complex journey: it takes them to the mysterious underworld realm of Demogorgon and ends in a dazzling "rebirth" of Asia, which must be understood, with respect to "a sea . . . of ever-spreading sound" (II, v, 84), as equivalent to the oceanic birth of Venus. All this (tellingly recapitulated in synesthetic terms by the final lyric of the act), especially in its passage from dark underworld to radiant rebirth, might be viewed as a happy version of Eurydice's story if we could imagine the Orphic music successfully descending into Hell and bringing her back to the light; structurally, it resembles the central description of the stream-of-sound in *Orpheus.* In Act III, after Prometheus's release from his rock and reunion with Asia, a liquid, sea-born music, blown from a "mystic shell" (iii, 70), envelops the whole earth, as though in an atmospheric "ocean" of sound, and effects a universal regeneration, comparable except for obvious differences in scale to Orpheus's transformation of desert to earthly paradise.

Act IV, commonly referred to as an "afterthought," joins to the plan of Acts I–III a cosmic vision in which Shelley floats a series of intricate apparitions on an uninterrupted stream-of-sound. (The phrase "stream of sound" appears twice here, in lines 505 and 506.) The consistency with which Shelley resumes and further develops his synesthetic scheme in this act deserves special notice. As we know with reference to both *Epipsychidion* and *Adonais,* critics have supposed that Shelley, under the spell of vagrant inspiration, could inartistically subjoin long "conclusions" to works already once concluded. In this they have been encouraged by the evidence, which no one cares to challenge, that this fourth act definitely is an afterpiece, composed some months after Acts I–III were completed. Obviously, whatever one's critical inclinations, the relationship between Act IV and the rest presents extraordinary opportunities for judging Shelley's qualities as a craftsman. A responsible decision in this matter must, I believe, give great weight to the last-act sequel to the stream-of-sound.

Before going on to details of this synesthetic scheme, I should like to comment briefly on several points that affect my treatment. Throughout, it will be necessary to remember that the stream-of-sound is only an aspect, though a very important one, of a complex system of imagery and symbolism. In details this system is severely demanding, as writers on the science and philosophy of *Prometheus Unbound* have shown.[10] But for convenience here its broad features can be described simply. Shelley's subject is no less than the fundamental nature and possibilities of physical and spiritual life. For physical life, as the extremely abundant imagery of clouds, rain, streams, and electrical phenomena constantly reminds us, the great sustaining force is the earth's atmosphere. For spiritual life the great sustaining force is love. Shelley characteristically treats each of these two creative forces as a manifold unity: the atmosphere is air and fire and moisture in all its forms, but remains the one "breath" of life (I, 177); love is "Gentleness, Virtue, Wisdom, and Endurance" (IV, 562)—sympathy, hope, imagination—but remains the one "Life of Life" (II, v, 48). Characteristically also, but in this poem supremely so, Shelley treats the atmosphere and love as though they were the two corresponding aspects of a single reality. This seems to me an essential clue to many difficulties of the imagery and symbolism in this often perplexing work. And it is what the synesthesia of *Prometheus Unbound* expresses more saliently and consistently than all else. In the stream-of-sound, stream must be associated with the atmosphere, even as I have already linked it with "dew," "spray," "vapors," "clouds," and "ocean" (and will link it, as in part previously also, with air and light or fire); sound, all harmonies, must be associated with love. But in addition, of course, stream and sound are synesthetically one. There are subtle interrelationships and ambiguities in all this which I will not pretend to cope with. For example, sound may be breath, an atmosphere itself; and its harmonies may actually be soundless, Pythagorean. But I believe the main currents and course of the stream-of-sound will be clear.

IV

In Shelley's version of the Prometheus story, the stream-of-sound has its role from beginning to end. At the opening of Act I the story is far advanced: Prometheus, bound to a precipice in the Indian Caucasus, has been Jupiter's victim for three thousand years. It is only well along in Act II, when Asia visits Demogorgon's cave, that we hear details of how the titan earned his chains by championing mankind against the divine tyrant. To a wasted earth and to "desert hearts" he brought such gifts as love and controlled fire (iv, 49–71); among these, emblematic of them all, was speech:

> He gave man speech, and speech created thought,
> Which is the measure of the universe;
> And Science struck the thrones of earth and heaven,
> Which shook, but fell not; and the harmonious mind
> Poured itself forth in all-prophetic song;
> And music lifted up the listening spirit
> Until it walked, exempt from mortal care,
> Godlike, o'er the clear billows of sweet sound.
> (iv, 72–79)

This harmonious stream was then parched, presumably, by Jupiter's bolts and Prometheus condemned to his rock.

Act I introduces us to a wasteland that recalls the scene of *Orpheus* as well as the world that Prometheus had once benevolently transformed: "Black, wintry, dead, unmeasured; without herb,/ Insect, or beast, or shape or sound of life" (21–22). One of Shelley's subtleties here is to show that Prometheus himself had helped toward this uncreation by becoming Jupiterlike in hate; another, related to this, is to show that the stream-of-sound may have a deadly opposite. Prometheus, soliloquizing, regrets having hated and cursed Jupiter; but when he says that he would "recall" (59) his curse, he equivocates, for it becomes plain that "recall" must mean both "revoke" and "entertain once again." He asks environmental personifications what that "thunder" (61 and 68) had been like. His apostrophe to "icy Springs" suggests that it had worse than silenced them (62–64). They confirm this by first describing how they had only "run mute" (80) amid the horrors of Jupiter's reign and then (in very poor verse, unfortunately) telling how, when they had carried it to "Indian waves," Prometheus's curse proved to have lethal effects (93–98). So much had Prometheus himself wanted "the harmonious mind." But these curse-laden springs are not further developed as a synesthetic device, nor do they form part of any systematically sustained opposition to the stream-of-sound. They only hint at their benign successor.

From this opening hint until near the close of the act the stream-of-sound is most notable by its absence. Prometheus's curse, with the ingenious dramatization of its repetition by a Phantasm of Jupiter, occupies close to a third of the whole act (about 250 lines of 833). Next follows an even more dominant movement (about 350 lines), in which

Mercury and a chorus of Furies afflict Prometheus with threats and temptations. Though Shelley suppresses his synesthetic scheme in these two sections of the act, he provides part of its background by establishing correspondences between physical and moral conditions, most clearly in speeches given to the Earth (especially 152–186), personified as Prometheus's mother. Hence it is fitting, when Prometheus has endured the Furies' utmost torture, that Earth should call up the comforting Spirits whose songs prelude the stream-of-sound (656ff.). These Spirits "inhabit" an atmosphere or "world-surrounding aether" which is "human thought" (658–661 and 675–676). They are described by Panthea and Ione, another sister of Asia, as gathering like vernal clouds and rising like fountain vapors, with a music suggestive of lake and waterfall (664–670). Ione, a little later, likens their voices to "despair/ Mingled with love and then dissolved in sound" (756–757), and Panthea, responding to this, leads us to infer that clouds and vapors have poured their music into one harmonious stream: "Canst thou speak, sister? all my words are drowned" (758).

Such are the slight but sure beginnings of the stream-of-sound in this act. Its flow is basic to the whole course of the next.

V

Act II is dominated by Venus symbolism, the chief character throughout being Asia, and the climax, in the last of five scenes, being her Venuslike rebirth. That Asia in this becomes or resembles a Venus Anadyomene cannot be doubted. But Shelley, I believe, wants us to see her as doubly Venusian, appearing at rebirth as a morning star. Certainly this "Child of Ocean," as she is frequently called at the beginning of the act (i, 170, 187, 194, 206), becomes in the climax a "Child of Light" (v, 54). It may be significant, incidentally, that "child of light" is a Spenserian epithet for Lucifer.[11] As a reborn Anadyomene, she has for parent ocean the stream-of-sound, and I believe Shelley meant his synesthetic stream in this act to bear light somewhat as its counterpart does in *Orpheus.* The light of the stream-of-sound here, which I take generally to be a stream-of-love, would most fittingly come from Shelley's favorite planet. He points clearly to this near the end of Act I, when a chorus of the Spirits that comfort Prometheus ask, "Hast thou beheld the form of Love?" and another Spirit answers:

As over wide dominions
I sped, like some swift cloud that wings the wide air's wildernesses,
That planet-crested shape swept by on lightning-braided pinions,
Scattering the liquid joy of life from his ambrosial tresses:
His footsteps paved the world with light. (763–767)

The masculine "shape" is Eros; his planet crest and light-bearing function mark him a Lucifer. But the love or "joy of life" which he scatters is "liquid," because here as elsewhere in *Prometheus Unbound,* as Notopoulos suggests, Shelley follows what Agathon says of Eros in the *Symposium:*[12] "He is then the youngest and the most delicate of all divinities; and in addition to this, he is, as it were, the most moist and liquid. For if he were otherwise, he could not, as he does, fold himself around everything, and secretly flow out and into every soul." [13] Love in the form of Eros, then, combines liquid with the light of the planet Venus.

And as Love in the form of Asia, to whom Eros is merely a forerunner, is Child both of Ocean and of Light, I think we have in her both Venus Anadyomene and Venus-Lucifer, reborn in both aspects from the stream-of-sound.

Scene i begins with a remarkable descriptive focus on the morning star. Asia, alone in a vale of the Indian Caucasus, awaits the coming of her sister Panthea. She speaks first of the spring season and its sudden coming to clothe "with golden clouds/ The desert of our life" (11–12). Then she continues:

> This is the season, this the day, the hour;
> At sunrise thou shouldst come, sweet sister mine,
> Too long desired, too long delaying, come!
> How like death-worms the wingless moments crawl!
> The point of one white star is quivering still
> Deep in the orange light of widening morn
> Beyond the purple mountains: through a chasm
> Of wind-divided mist the darker lake
> Reflects it: now it wanes: it gleams again
> As the waves fade, and as the burning threads
> Of woven cloud unravel in pale air:
> 'Tis lost! and through yon peaks of cloud-like snow
> The roseate sunlight quivers: hear I not
> The Aeolian music of her sea-green plumes
> Winnowing the crimson dawn? (13–27)

I have quoted this at length and as a unit for several reasons. Asia's intense concentration on the fading of Venus's "white star" (17) is notably Shelleyan. So are her enumeration of rainbow colors, from crimson to purple, and her reference to Aeolian music. She has, in short, brought together the three principal foci of Shelley's synesthesia and carefully underscored at least two of them, the morning star and the spectrum. The passage contains no synesthetic image, not even in its last three lines, which have a certain notoriety in discussions of Shelley's intersense analogies.[14] But it may be said to contain an eminently synesthetic *situation,* especially if we see Asia on this occasion as a typical visionary and Panthea as a typical apparition. Taking this passage alone and thinking of similar situations in Shelley's visionary verse, especially in *Alastor* and *The Triumph of Life,* I suppose that Panthea's Aeolian music has brought a heavenly rainbow harmony down to earth and that its sounding at the very instant when the star vanishes suggests Panthea herself to be a descended Venus. The latter guess appears to be confirmed by what Asia adds as Panthea enters:

I feel, I see
Those eyes which burn through smiles that fade in tears,
Like stars half quenched in mists of silver dew. (27–29)

Since Asia both *feels* and *sees* Panthea's starlike eyes, whereas Shelley in the *Skylark* and Rousseau in *The Triumph of Life* could feel, but hardly or not at all see, the faded morning star, it is pertinent to emphasize that Panthea's arrival begins no ordinary day. It heralds the Promethean day of love's triumph, in which Venus's heavenly influence will not wane after dawn. But if Panthea here is an almost wholly revealed Venus, complications in scene v of this act may indicate that she can be so only to a greater Venus, Asia herself.

After a remarkable passage (i, 71–86) which recalls love between Panthea and the self-redeemed, glorious Prometheus in terms of atmospheric evaporation and condensation, in scenes i–iii the gradually gathering stream-of-sound bears Panthea and Asia from the Indian vale to the weird realm of Demogorgon. First, Asia is stimulated by signs in a dream, especially by a mysterious command to "follow." When she cries out in bewilderment, Echoes repeat, "Follow, Follow!" (i, 162). These Echoes are compared to dew, and their "liquid responses" urge Asia, "Child of Ocean," to pursue their receding song as it floats toward shadowy depths and sinks on the ebbing wind (166–208). In scene ii semichoruses of spirits report Asia's and Panthea's progress through a forest whose depths can be pierced only by clouds of dew and rainlike drops of golden starlight (ii, 1–23). Within this forest there is an "overflow" of the song of nightingales and of the sound made by their rushing wings (24–40). The sounds, somewhat oddly but suggestively, are likened to the music of "many a lake-surrounded flute" (38). And all these tributary currents of the stream-of-sound swell forth in one of the semichoruses:

> There those enchanted eddies play
> Of echoes, music-tongued, which draw,
> By Demogorgon's mighty law,
> With melting rapture, or sweet awe,
> All spirits on that secret way;
> As inland boats are driven to Ocean
> Down streams made strong with mountain-thaw:
> And first there comes a gentle sound
> To those in talk or slumber bound,
> And wakes the destined soft emotion,—
> Attracts, impels them; those who saw
> Say from the breathing earth behind
> There steams a plume-uplifting wind
> Which drives them on their path, while they
> Believe their own swift wings and feet

The sweet desires within obey:
And so they float upon their way,
Until, still sweet, but loud and strong,
The storm of sound is driven along,
Sucked up and hurrying: as they fleet
Behind, its gathering billows meet
And to the fatal mountain bear
Like clouds amid the yielding air. (41–63)

This journey to the "fatal mountain" in Demogorgon's realm is completed by the opening of scene iii, in the first line of which Panthea announces: "Hither the sound has borne us." She and Asia find themselves on a rocky pinnacle, "islanded" in a sea of billowing clouds, while all about them the mountains echo to the fall of sun-loosened avalanches of snow (1–42). Whelmed in this cloudy sea, the two Oceanids hear spirits bidding them follow a downward whirl of sounds (43–98). In scene iv the pair at length reach Demogorgon's cave, and Asia questions this dark power about God, man, and mutability, and about Prometheus's destined release (1–128). She learns that all things remain subject to fate, time, occasion, chance, and change except "eternal Love." At the close of the interview she beholds a terrifying charioteer about to conduct to Jupiter's precarious throne the car of that Hour which augurs doom to the old tyrannical order (129–155). She and Panthea then enter the chariot of another Hour, herald of the Promethean era. This chariot, which will bear Asia to her Venuslike rebirth, is portrayed aptly as an "ivory shell" (157).

In scene v the sisters ascend in the chariot to a mountain-capping cloud, and here Panthea and the Hour behold Asia transfigured. She becomes brilliant as sunlight, the sun itself being yet unrisen, and her presence is felt rather than seen. And now Panthea, recalling Asia's original birth from the sea, likens this transfiguration to it:

> The Nereids tell
> That on the day when the clear hyaline
> Was cloven at thine uprise, and thou didst stand
> Within a veinèd shell, which floated on
> Over the calm floor of the crystal sea,
> Among the Aegean isles, and by the shores
> Which bear thy name; love, like the atmosphere
> Of the sun's fire filling the living world,
> Burst from thee, and illumined earth and heaven
> And the deep ocean and the sunless caves
> And all that dwells within them; till grief cast
> Eclipse upon the soul from which it came:
> Such art thou now. (20–32)

In so presenting Asia's radiant, shell-borne, Luciferlike regeneration, Shelley plainly strives to fuse qualities of Venus Anadyomene with those of Venus the morning star. And Asia's Venusian ascendancy over Panthea (felt, *un*seen —line 17) must look back tellingly to the felt-seen apparition of the latter which opened this act.

The stream-of-sound motif, somewhat muted for a while, is now restored and sustained to the end of the act. Spirits sing in unison the love which all feel for Asia, now "Child of Light" (48–71). She responds in a long lyric, "My soul is an enchanted boat" (72–110), which should be read in entirety for its detailed restatement of the synesthetic motif. The lyric ends the act and sums up the movement of the stream-of-sound, which started with the dewlike Echoes in scene i. Like a boat on the "silver waves" of a universal love-hymn, Asia floats down a winding river until reaching "a sea profound, of ever-spreading sound" (72–84). Still driven on by music, she glides among Elysian islands in

> Realms where the air we breathe is love,
> Which in the winds and on the waves doth move,
> Harmonizing this earth with what we feel above.
> (95–97)

The theme of rebirth is also stated once again, this time in a brief allegory, which represents the voyage as a safe passage to the paradise of a new day, through perils of Age, Manhood, Youth, Infancy, and Death-and-Birth, in that Plato-echoing order (98–110).[15] The voyage concludes with a vision of glorious shapes walking on the sea and chanting.

Such, then, in rude outline, is the development and recapitulation of the stream-of-sound motif in Act II. Shelley's presentation of it undoubtedly offers difficulties (there appear, for example, to be streams within streams),[16] but the general direction and meaning of his water-sound symbolism, dominated by Asia-Venus's rebirth, emerge clearly enough. And only in Act IV does Shelley devote equal pains to elaborating a complex pattern of harmonious agencies in streaming sound.

VI

In Act III the role of the stream-of-sound, mainly associated with a marvelous sea shell, is major but needs only brief explication. Music, especially sea-music, sounds as it were throughout the act, but synesthetic imagery is relatively scarce and the millennial effects of the shell's harmonies are recounted rather generally in the last two of four scenes.

Scene i briefly presents the fall of Jupiter, which necessarily follows Asia's rebirth. Foreseeing another birth, fruit of his embrace with the sea nymph Thetis, which should seal his dominion over mankind, Jupiter exultantly calls on his cupbearer to pour a libation:

> Pour forth heaven's wine, Idaean Ganymede,
> And let it fill the Daedal cups like fire,
> And from the flower-inwoven soil divine
> Ye all-triumphant harmonies arise,
> As dew from earth under the twilight stars.
> (25–29)

This is thoroughly ironic. Jupiter's "offspring" is really his nemesis, Demogorgon. And not Ganymede but another sort of cupbearer will diffuse humid harmonies over earth, making it a "soil divine." Scene ii, again quite briefly, presents Apollo and Ocean commenting on Jupiter's fall and foretelling universal concord. Shelley here puts markedly coordinate emphases on the "azure calm" of Ocean's domain and the music which will invest it. But he does not employ intersense analogies to recall the synesthetic scheme, unless Ocean's famous line on his sounding waves should be taken for a hint:

> It is the unpastured sea hungering for calm. (49)

Scene iii, telling of Prometheus's reunion with Asia and of Earth's rejuvenation, again stresses music associated with the sea. We hear, for example, that Asia's sister Ione will assuage the hardly concealed dread of paradisal monotony by chanting "fragments of sea-music" (27). But it is the marvelous shell that unmistakably re-establishes the stream-of-sound. The shell, Proteus's wedding gift to Asia ages before, had been safely hidden during Jupiter's tyranny. Recovered now, it is described by Ione as an obviously synesthetic instrument:

> this is the mystic shell;
> See the pale azure fading into silver
> Lining it with a soft yet glowing light:
> Looks it not like lulled music sleeping there?
> (70–73)[17]

This Prometheus orders to be given to the Hour of his triumph, a kind of Ganymede who will bear it about the world, "Loosening its mighty music" (81). In the remainder of this scene, while Earth describes how she and all her children will henceforth regain joy and peace through Orphic transfigurations, we must imagine that Asia's shell, its "lulled music" now awakened as she herself is reborn, bathes the world in its oceanic harmonies. The symbolism of all this was nicely summed up by G. Wilson Knight: "Its music is the love-music, foam-born, to be now felt flooding the dry arteries of Earth." [18]

Description of the shell's effects takes up much of the concluding scene (iv, 54–204). To grasp concisely their relationship to the stream-of-sound, we should recall what was said earlier of earth's atmosphere and love and of Plato's moist Eros, for the Hour now epitomizes all in reporting back to Prometheus:

> Soon as the sound had ceased whose thunder filled
> The abysses of the sky and the wide earth,
> There was a change: the impalpable thin air
> And the all-circling sunlight were transformed,

> As if the sense of love dissolved in them
> Had folded itself round the spherèd world.
> (98–103)

Thus, as lethal thunders dominated the opening of Act I, rocking and racking the "orbèd world" (I, 69), so now a vitalizing thunder leaves the "spherèd world" enveloped with love. And the stream-of-sound, having originated in Act I in clouds and fountain vapors, has become at the end of Act III a new kind of all-embracing Oceanus.

VII

Between Shelley's completion of Act III and composition of Act IV he wrote one extended work, *The Cenci,* which differs decidedly in character from his lyrical drama. Publishing *The Cenci* as a play definitely meant for the stage, Shelley declared in his preface that he had decorously fixed severe curbs on its imagery.[19] And the change from profusion of imagery in *Prometheus Unbound* to the restraint of *The Cenci* is itself indeed dramatic. Yet we should be quite wrong, I believe, to infer from this that Shelley was somehow recoiling from indulgence to discipline, rather than adjusting to different economies. Coming after *The Cenci* and reverting essentially to the style of earlier portions of *Prometheus Unbound,* Act IV invites us to see, not some relapse from control into laxness, but distinct management of artistic means. What in fact may be considered most striking about Shelley's imagery in this epilogue is his obviously conscious maintenance of patterns which appear in Acts I–III, along with resumption of their symbolic overtones. Certainly, stream-of-sound imagery abounds in the conclusion and has structural functions closely comparable to those in Act II. Again, this imagery continues to support Shelley's themes of love and harmony in man and the universe. The stream-of-sound, in short, flows through the entire poem, and its prolongation in Act IV not only assures consistency of poetic design but strengthens, as well as extends, unifying patterns of the whole.

In the single cosmic scene of Act IV, it is customary to distinguish three movements, but no one has observed how the stream-of-sound presents and orders them. Throughout the act, two characters, Panthea and Ione, serve as witnesses, or auditors, and as partial interpreters of events. They first hear choruses of Spirits and Hours celebrating renewals of love and harmony in the Promethean era (1–179). In the second movement they describe two visions, of Moon and of Earth, and then listen to the antiphonal singing of planet and satellite (194–502). At last, Panthea and Ione behold the rise of Demogorgon and are among the hearers of his universally significant announcement of Prometheus's triumph, qualified by eternally threatening evil (510–578). It is in transitions from movement to movement of this three-fold scheme that the structural bearings of the stream-of-sound most clearly emerge.

Echoes of the stream-of-sound occur throughout the first movement and answer to its symbolic overtones in Acts I–III. Singing Spirits, born of the "deep," are called forth to gather as clouds in heaven, as dew-stars on earth, or as "Waves assemble on ocean" (42), and they respond to Hope, Love, and Power, "As the billows leap in the morning beams!" (68). The world in which these elemental Spirits pursue their cycle is a microcosm, man's mind, which now resembles a serenely moving ocean (93–98). Spirits and Hours chant the fulfillment of their being:

Then weave the web of the mystic measure;
From the depths of the sky and the ends of the earth,
Come, swift Spirits of might and of pleasure,
Fill the dance and the music of mirth,
As the waves of a thousand streams rush by
To an ocean of splendour and harmony! (129–134)

With man reformed, the Spirits freely exert their harmonizing influence in universal wanderings. One semichorus of Hours accompanies them, while the other encircles the earth, changing all to its music. Whatever their path, all Spirits and Hours lead on "clouds that are heavy with love's sweet rain" (179).

The first movement ends thus in a final chorus of Spirits and Hours. In a brief transition to the second movement, Shelley plainly reveals that the whole of the first was itself a stream of harmony. In the momentary silence following the chorus, Ione asks Panthea if she feels no delight in the "past sweetness" (180–181), and the answer implies that the music had been a rain of melody. Panthea says she delights in memory of the song,

As the bare green hill
When some soft cloud vanishes into rain,
Laughs with a thousand drops of sunny water
To the unpavilioned sky! (181–184)

The second movement, dealing with Moon and Earth, is one of the most discussed sections in all of Shelley's poetry. Its allusions to various scientific theories have attracted especial notice, and have been most thoroughly explored by Grabo.[20] The baffling description of the sphere of Earth in one passage has been taken as an extreme instance of all that is most perplexing in *Prometheus Un-*

bound.[21] And this description includes what is probably Shelley's best-known attempt to give an idea of ultimate unity through synesthetic expression.[22] But intersense analogies figure importantly from beginning to end of this difficult movement.

Its opening, like the transition just before, implies that all here is borne along synesthetically. Panthea and Ione hear new notes succeed to those of the Spirits and Hours—first, the profound bass of the Earth, then higher tones of the Moon—together, a kind of spheral harmony:

Panthea. 'Tis the deep music of the rolling world
Kindling within the strings of the waved air
Aeolian modulations.

Ione. Listen too,
How every pause is filled with under-notes,
Clear, silver, icy, keen, awakening tones,
Which pierce the sense, and live within the soul,
As the sharp stars pierce winter's crystal air
And gaze upon themselves within the sea. (186–193)

These star-sharp, multiply synesthetic tones, as is soon evident, are really a further reach of the stream-of-sound, and they actually produce the two "visions" of Moon and Earth which Ione and Panthea respectively describe. Here is how Panthea "visualizes" their strange synesthetic crystallization:

> But see where through two openings in the forest
> Which hanging branches overcanopy,
> And where two runnels of a rivulet,
> Between the close moss violet-inwoven,
> Have made their path of melody . . . ;

Two visions of strange radiance float upon
The ocean-like enchantment of strong sound,
Which flows intenser, keener, deeper yet
Under the ground and through the windless air.
(194–205)

Within the descriptions of the visions, moreover, we find added evidence of their origin in "The ocean-like enchantment of strong sound." For example, the Moon appears in a boatlike chariot, and as this passes from Ione's view its wheels "wake sounds,/ Sweet as a singing rain of silver dew" (234–235). But the swirling involutions of the stream-of-sound become most complex in Panthea's vision of the sphere of Earth. She beholds it rolling out of the forest, surfaced on one of those "two runnels of a rivulet." It rushes out "with loud and whirlwind harmony," much like Milton's Chariot of Paternal Deity:[23]

A sphere, which is as many thousand spheres,
Solid as crystal, yet through all its mass
Flow, as through empty space, music and light:
Ten thousand orbs involving and involved,
Purple and azure, white, and green, and golden,
Sphere within sphere. . . . (238–243)

Here it should be remarked specially how Shelley sets forth the colors within the sphere. With the exception of white, the colors ranged in a single line appear in inverse order to the spectral red, orange, yellow, green, blue, indigo, and violet. And it is apparent that their range, from golden to purple, completes a stylized spectrum. Now if the central white may be taken to indicate a source or focus of pure light, from which the colors bend to their prismatic extremes, Shelley has given in this line a verbal diagram of the spectral phenomena which he so favors in his vision themes and their synesthetic expression. In the present scientific, symbolic vision of intervolved orbs and flowing light and music, it looks as though Shelley has chosen a peculiarly apt way to recall Newton's analogy between the spectrum bands and the octave intervals. The obvious spirit of Panthea's whole description is to express unity in multiplicity, and here light and music must participate in that unity.

As Panthea's account continues, its synesthetic symbolism develops and relates unmistakably to the over-all motif of the stream of harmony:

> With mighty whirl the multitudinous orb
> Grinds the bright brook into an azure mist
> Of elemental subtlety, like light;
> And the wild odour of the forest flowers,
> The music of the living grass and air,
> The emerald light of leaf entangled beams
> Round its intense yet self-conflicting speed,
> Seem kneaded into one aëreal mass
> Which drowns the sense. (253–261)

These verses, presenting in the context of the act and the poem a synesthetic *ne plus ultra,* may be construed best with steady focus on the presumed "psychology" of their narrator. Panthea envisions the complex unity of the orb as a harmony within the stream-of-sound; the brook which the orb transmutes is itself part of this stream; and the total synesthesia of the "aëreal mass" is brought surely into the comprehensive scheme because, like some great wave, it *drowns* her perception.

Nothing in the rest of this second movement rivals the complexity of Panthea's imaginative model of harmonious unity. She next sees visions of a Spirit within the sphere, and of geological and historical strata, X-rayed by starbeams from the Spirit's forehead. These visions concluded, Earth and Moon begin their duet, singing the changes effected in them by omnipotent love. From Earth, a flamelike spirit pierces the Moon with "love, and odour, and deep melody" (330), endowing the frozen globe with a life-sustaining atmosphere and converting it into a miniature earth. To Earth, the Moon's light and voice become a balm of "crystal accents" (499). One passage of this duet, sung by Earth, reasserts the basic human theme of the drama, which will be given final statement by Demogorgon in the next movement: Man, we hear, has become a "sea reflecting love," no longer shadowed by fear, hate, pain; he is:

> one harmonious soul of many a soul,
> Whose nature is its own divine control,
> Where all things flow to all, as rivers to the sea.
> (400–402)

Following this long second movement are the transitional comments of Panthea and Ione that once again remind us that all has been borne on the stream-of-sound. When the visions and the duet are past, they say:

> *Panthea.* I rise as from a bath of sparkling water,
> A bath of azure light, among dark rocks,
> Out of the stream of sound.
>
> *Ione.* Ah me! sweet sister,
> The stream of sound has ebbed away from us,
> And you pretend to rise out of its wave,
> Because your words fall like the clear, soft dew
> Shaken from a bathing wood-nymph's limbs and hair.
> (503–509)

The last and shortest movement is devoted to Demogorgon's apocalyptic tidings, made from the viewpoint of eternity. He proclaims the victory of Prometheus, of Gentleness, Virtue, Wisdom, and Endurance. But he also warns against the eternal danger of refluent evil and chaos. In his vast perspective, even the Promethean, cosmic stream of harmony can but jet against the night of time. And Demogorgon's very appearance to Panthea and Ione suggests a darkly streaming background to what they have witnessed and to events of the whole poem:

> A mighty Power, which is as darkness,
> Is rising out of Earth, and from the sky
> Is showered like night, and from within the air
> Bursts, like eclipse which had been gathered up
> Into the pores of sunlight: the bright visions,
> Wherein the singing spirits rode and shone,
> Gleam like pale meteors through a watery night.
> (510–516)

This dark shower, comprehending the Dantesque singing meteors of visions, is the "universal sound" of Demogorgon's fateful words (517–518). And this, rather than any power of Jupiter, is the contrast, or ground, for the streaming harmony which flows with freest volume after the Promethean triumph. Demogorgon neither "eclipses" the triumph nor drowns out the stream-of-sound. His Power sets out the eternal conditions in which both are possible.

7

CONCLUSION

Writing to Godwin close to the middle of his career (December 1817), Shelley sketched what he took to be his special, though imperfectly realized, imaginative bent: he thought himself particularly fitted "to apprehend minute and remote distinctions of feeling, whether relative to external nature or the living beings which surround us, and to communicate the conceptions which result from considering either the moral or the material universe as a whole." [1] This, in my opinion, pithily summarizes his two essential, complementary aims as a psychological and philosophical (or religious, or myth-making) poet—to record on the one hand delicately discriminated sensory, emotional, and moral perceptions; and on the other to comprehend even the finest, least common observations and insights within a synthesis of human awareness. Appreciation of these aims, while strengthening one's grasp of

Shelley's entire work, is indispensable in tackling the most intense, ambitious shapings of his peculiar vision—such ideal poems as have engrossed this study. And these aims to relate the most subtle to the most sweeping yield basic clues to Shelley's cunning with synesthesia in the earliest as well as the latest among his "visionary rhymes."

How fitly synesthesia served Shelley's aims in ideal contexts can be inferred from certain presumptive grounds of his practice, which fundamentally entails belief in some system of intersense analogies. Such analogies, considered individually, basically represent, or arise from, heightened normal perception, though they may at times seem distinctly supranormal or even perverse; in any case, they constitute a species of "minute and remote" discriminations. But theoretically at least, these intersense analogies fall into regular patterns (as implied, for example, in the spectrum-gamut parallel), which suggest that they all contribute to a comprehensive "harmony" of the senses. Hence in regard to both particular perceptions and their implied synthesis, the theory of intersense analogy presumed by Shelley's practice shows how nicely his synesthesia accorded with the imaginative idiosyncrasies of his own shrewd analysis.

But apart from such hypothetical reconstruction, one can summarize confidently enough how Shelley's synesthesia subserved the primary designs of his ideal verse. That he customarily associated intersense analogies with highly refined, even quasi-mystical, perception is manifest as early as *The Retrospect* and *Queen Mab,* and is overwhelmingly evident in such later poems as *Alastor, Epipsychidion,* and *The Triumph of Life.* In these and similar works Shelley used synesthesia most clearly and consistently to provide instances and emblems of superfine awareness in contexts which usher in vision figures, like the fairy Mab, the veiled maiden of *Alastor*, or similar embodiments of ideal qualities. In such contexts, moreover, especially those of his most mature art, Shelley characteristically strives to achieve effects of some straining confrontation with a very complicated, even paradoxical, unity, barely perceived (felt, unseen), yet overpowering. These effects radiate to every level of perception, but at the same time tend to diminish or obliterate ordinary distinctions between, for example, the sensory and the spiritual. And to produce such effects, synesthesia proved to be one of Shelley's aptest devices, not only because it combined delicate sensory discriminations with intimations of total sensory harmony, but also because visionary synesthetic perception could be made to betoken spiritual elevation and order.

The general symbolic value of Shelley's synesthesia, like that of Dante's, derives from his equation of sensory perception with moral discernment, so that synesthetic acuteness and the harmony of the senses reflect corresponding keenness and consonance of moral awareness. This, of course, merely extends or varies such common symbolic relationships as that between physical and spiritual vision, but Shelley's equation has at least two extremely interesting implications. First, we should consider that, for Shelley, synesthetic perception was an especially vivid earnest, not simply a sign, of harmonious development of the whole human personality; that is, as already suggested, his synesthesia involves a coordination, or even a fusion, of sensuous and spiritual experience. (For brief but telling illustration, recall the Pythagorean-Dantesque variant in "The sphere whose light is melody to lovers.") Then, also, his synesthesia helps to focus our attention, not on the apparent otherworldliness of his visionary ideals, but generally on the act of vision itself, and specifically on its inclusiveness and intricacy.

These observations about Shelley's synesthesia, its symbolism and its relationship to his special imaginative endeavors, bear, of course, on questions which concern less strictly literary aspects of his work. His metaphysical and aesthetic views, for example, have fairly obvious connections with the principles that must be supposed, in part at least, to have shaped his synesthetic practice. That practice, as interpreted here, reveals a sustained, consistent effort to discover and celebrate values inherent in the coordinate expansion and sharpening of all human faculties, the whole trend of this development being dominated by love, or imaginative sympathy. For Shelley, any "final" answer about the true, the good, and the beautiful would not be likely to require denial or drastic revision of such values. Not extravagantly, at any rate, one may submit that his steady elaboration of synesthetic themes in his most intensely philosophical contexts points up sharply a concern, not to escape the "material" and the sensuous, but to test and demonstrate how one order of experience can relate to other and supposedly higher ones.

But it was never my aspiration here to explore such abstruse matters. The primary intention throughout has been simply to bring to notice how resourcefully and responsibly Shelley exploited synesthesia. And while nothing appears more radically evident and significant about his synesthetic practice than the futility which must beset every effort to assess it as an isolated device—to pull it out of contexts, or weigh its meaning apart from the cumulative meaning of entire poems—nevertheless one can describe with some assurance those very features which mainly bespeak its participation in organic entities. These are the recurrence of his intersense analogies in patterns and the close relationship of such patterns to certain symbols and to symbolic motifs. Sympathetic attention to these features of Shelley's synesthesia should promote a rather better opinion than has been fashionable of his artistic handling of language, image, and symbol.

Finally, it should be challenged for him that no other poet matches Shelley's care and ingenuity in working synesthesia into the fabric of his verse. His titles in this respect derive from (1) the variety of ways in which he adapted synesthetic imagery to symbolic themes, (2) his success in sustaining and elaborating synesthetic motifs as part of basic structures of entire poems, and (3) his persistent, fresh resort to synesthesia in one after another of his most characteristic major works. Dante may have provided his great model and much of his encouragement in all this, but Shelley's synesthesia is proportionally more impressive than Dante's; and though, ultimately, that in *The Divine Comedy* must be ranged with nothing similar for imaginative magnificence, Shelley's works display a synesthesia more intricately symbolic and formally subtle. Other poets may yield a far higher "count" of synesthetic images than Shelley's; some may considerably surpass him in conferring psychological plausibility on uncommon intersense analogies. Few others, however, can have glimpsed the possibilities he saw to develop synesthesia from a more or less casual device into a complex, powerful artistic instrument. And no poet, not even Baudelaire, I believe, has rivaled Shelley in steady, diverse, refined experiment with these possibilities.

NOTES

Chapter 1

[1] E.g., William Empson, *Seven Types of Ambiguity*, 2nd edn., London, 1947, pp. 12–14.

[2] Neville Rogers, *Shelley at Work: A Critical Inquiry*, Oxford, 1956; Milton Wilson, *Shelley's Later Poetry: A Study of His Prophetic Imagination*, New York, 1959; Harold Bloom, *Shelley's Mythmaking*, New Haven, 1959. Bloom's one reference to synesthesia (pp. 116–117) seems trifling; see Chap. 6, note 14. Wilson (pp. 37–38) gives an interesting, unfavorable analysis of Shelley's synesthetic lyric *The Keen Stars Were Twinkling*, written in 1822.

[3] "Synästhesien in der englischen Dichtung des 19. Jahrhunderts: Ein ästhetisch-psychologischer Versuch" (*Englische Studien*, 53 [1919–1920], 1–157; 196–334), pp. 223–246.

[4] *The Imagery of Keats and Shelley: A Comparative Study*, Chapel Hill, 1949, pp. 101–138.

[5] Downey, "Literary Synesthesia," *Journal of Philosophy, Psychology, and Scientific Methods*, 9 (1912), 490–498; Firkins, *Power and Elusiveness in Shelley*, Minneapolis, 1937, pp. 136–144. Deserving mention also is S. J. Mary Suddard, *Keats, Shelley and Shakespeare: Studies and Essays in English Literature*, Cambridge, Eng., 1912, pp. 100–108.

[6] Miss Downey's chapter, "The Concordance of the Senses," in her *Creative Imagination: Studies in the Psychology of Literature*, New York, 1929, pp. 93–104, agrees substantially with the

1912 article; I shall cite both as representative of her early research.

[7] *The New Laokoon: An Essay on the Confusion of the Arts,* Boston and New York, 1910.

[8] Babbitt, p. 183.

[9] "Literary Synesthesia" as a whole aims at this distinction; cf. "The Concordance of the Senses," pp. 94, 100–101.

[10] "Literary Synesthesia," p. 492; "The Concordance of the Senses," p. 96.

[11] "The Concordance of the Senses," pp. 100–101; "synaesthesia" is the spelling adopted in *Creative Imagination.*

[12] *The Sensitive Plant,* I, 27–28. All quotations of Shelley's verse and of prose regularly printed therewith (e.g., prefaces and notes of Shelley and Mary) are from *The Complete Poetical Works of Percy Bysshe Shelley,* ed. Thomas Hutchinson, in the Oxford Standard Authors Series, London, Oxford University Press, as reset in 1934 and often reprinted. (Hutchinson's edn. was first published by the Clarendon Press, Oxford, 1904.) This will be cited hereafter as *PW*. Other Shelley prose, including correspondence, is quoted from *The Complete Works of Percy Bysshe Shelley,* Julian edn., ed. Roger Ingpen and Walter E. Peck, 10 vols., London and New York, 1926–1930; cited hereafter as *JW*.

[13] "Literary Synesthesia," pp. 491, 496; "The Concordance of the Senses," pp. 100–101.

[14] Erhardt-Siebold, p. 224: "*Shelley ist der erste Dichter in der englischen Literatur, der konsequent die Synästhesien gebraucht* —er ist ihr Hauptvertreter im 19. Jahrhundert geblieben. Wohl begegnet man Synästhesien, selbst in grosser Zahl, noch bei andern Dichtern. Aber Shelleys Stil kommt dem wahren Wesen der Synästhesien am nächsten."

[15] Erhardt-Siebold, pp. 43ff.

[16] See Albert Wellek, "Das Doppelempfinden im abendländischen Altertum und Mittelalter," *Archiv für die gesamte Psychologie,* 80 (1931), 120–166; idem, "Renaissance- und Barock-Synästhesie: Die Geschichte des Doppelempfindens im 16. und 17. Jahrhundert," *Deutsche Vierteljahrsschrift für Literaturwissenschaft und Geistesgeschichte,* 9 (1931), 534–584; William B. Stanford, *Greek Metaphor: Studies in Theory and Practice,* Oxford, 1936, pp. 47–61; Alfred G. Engstrom, "In Defence of Synaesthesia in

Literature," *PQ*, 25 (1946), 1–19; Stephen Ullmann, *The Principles of Semantics*, Glasgow, 1951, pp. 266–289.

[17] Erhardt-Siebold, p. 333.

[18] *Les Fleurs du Mal*, "Toute Entière."

[19] Erhardt-Siebold, pp. 224–230.

[20] Erhardt-Siebold, pp. 243–246. Mrs. von Erhardt-Siebold later wrote an English summary of her work on synesthesia, "Harmony of the Senses in English, German, and French Romanticism," *PMLA*, 47 (1932), 577–592.

[21] Firkins, p. 3.

[22] Firkins, p. 136.

[23] Firkins, p. 136. Dante's phrase, which is not "applied to sunset," appears in *Inferno*, I, 60.

[24] Firkins, pp. 140–142.

[25] Firkins, p. 143.

[26] Fogle, pp. 101-102.

[27] Fogle, p. 137.

[28] Fogle, pp. 136–137.

[29] Fogle, pp. 123, 127, 122.

[30] Fogle, pp. 137–138.

[31] Fogle, p. 105.

[32] Fogle, pp. 134–136.

[33] Cf. J. Isaacs, *The Background of Modern Poetry*, New York, 1958, pp. 31–33.

[34] See Newman I. White, ed., *The Unextinguished Hearth: Shelley and His Contemporary Critics*, Durham, N. C., 1938, pp. 223, 243–246 (*Prometheus Unbound*); 277–281 (*Epipsychidion*); 288–289, 293, 295–296 (*Adonais*).

[35] *The Unextinguished Hearth*, pp. 277–278; review in *The Gossip*, July 14, 1821.

[36] *The Unextinguished Hearth*, p. 288.

[37] *The Unextinguished Hearth*, p. 245; review (October, 1821) of Shelley's *Prometheus Unbound* volume. Hill and Helen C. Shine, *The Quarterly Review under Gifford: Identification of Contributors, 1809–1824*, Chapel Hill, 1949, p. 76, identify the reviewer as William S. Walker.

[38] *The Unextinguished Hearth*, p. 246.

[39] *JW*, VII, 111.

[40] *JW*, VII, 115.

[41] *De l'Allemagne*, ed. Jean de Pange, 5 vols., Paris, 1958–1960, IV, 246–248; my trans.

[42] *Opticks*, Book II, Part I, Obs. 14; Part IV, Obs. 5 and 8; citations from the modern reprint (ed. E. T. Whittaker, New York, 1931) of the 4th edn. (1730).

[43] "Das Doppelempfinden im 18. Jahrhundert" (*Deutsche Vierteljahrsschrift f. Literaturwiss. und Geistesgesch.*, 14 [1936], 75–102), p. 77. See also Marjorie H. Nicolson, *Newton Demands the Muse*, Princeton, 1946, pp. 65n and 85ff.

[44] *An Essay concerning Human Understanding* (III, iv, 11), ed. Alexander C. Fraser, 2 vols., Oxford, 1894, II, 38. For comment on the blind man, including Mme. de Staël's erroneous identification see Kenneth MacLean, *John Locke and English Literature of the Eighteenth Century*, New Haven, 1936, pp. 106ff.; and Nicolson, *op. cit.* p. 84n.

[45] Steele, *The Tatler*, No. 227 (1710); Fielding, *Tom Jones*, Bk. IV, Ch. i, and Bk. VI, Ch. i; Johnson, *The Rambler*, No. 94 (1751).

[46] "Zur Geschichte und Kritik der Synästhesie-Forschung" (*Archiv f. d. ges. Psych.*, 79 [1931], 325–384), p. 329.

[47] *The Botanic Garden*, 2 vols., 4th edn., London, 1799, p. 181; further reference to Darwin will be made later in this chapter.

[48] Anthony, Earl of Shaftesbury, *Second Characters, or The Language of Forms*, ed. Benjamin Rand, Cambridge, Eng., 1914, pp. 148–149. For a fresh consideration of the blind man, see the reference to Empson, *Seven Types of Ambiguity*, in note 1 above.

[49] Indispensable for study of Castel is Donald S. Schier, *Louis Bertrand Castel, Anti-Newtonian Scientist*, Cedar Rapids, Iowa, 1941; pp. 133–196 give a thorough treatment of the theory, practice, and influence, of Castel's color organ.

[50] In discussing the plan of his invention, Castel said that it had been inspired by a passage in Athanasius Kircher, *Musurgia Universalis*, Rome, 1650 (Schier, p. 136).

[51] Schier, p. 152.

[52] In his *Éléments de la Philosophie de Newton* (1738), chapter XIV, Voltaire described Castel's proposed invention with reserved, possibly ironic, approval; the relevant passage was later suppressed, however, and Voltaire changed his name for the in-

ventor from "Euclide-Castel" to that given above. See *Oeuvres Complètes de Voltaire,* 52 vols., Paris, 1877–1885, XXII, 503–506.

[53] *The Loves of the Plants,* Interlude III, following Canto III; for quotations, I have used *The Botanic Garden,* 2 vols., 4th edn., London, 1799, in which Interlude III appears on pp. 167–186 of vol. II. *The Temple of Nature,* Section III, entitled "Melody of Colours," of "Additional Note XIII, Analysis of Taste."

[54] *The Botanic Garden,* II, 178–179.

[55] *The Botanic Garden,* II, 179.

[56] *The Botanic Garden,* II, 179–180.

[57] *The Botanic Garden,* II, 180–181.

[58] *The Botanic Garden,* II, 181. In *The Temple of Nature,* the section on "Melody of Colours" substantially restates what has been reviewed above, but perhaps gives greatest emphasis to Robert's findings on ocular spectra; referring again to the possibility of a color organ, Darwin does not mention Castel.

[59] For Walker's activities at Syon House and Eton and for his general influence on Shelley, see Newman I. White, *Shelley,* 2 vols., New York, 1940, I, 22–24, 40; Kenneth N. Cameron, *The Young Shelley: Genesis of a Radical,* New York, 1950, pp. 8, 80, 294; and, most recently, Desmond King-Hele, *Shelley: His Thought and Work,* London, 1960, pp. 158–159.

[60] Walker, *A System of Familiar Philosophy: In Twelve Lectures,* 2 vols., London, 1802, II, 90. (An earlier, one-vol. edn. of this work appeared in 1799.)

[61] Walker, II, 90.

[62] Walker, II, 91.

[63] Walker, II, 125.

[64] King-Hele, p. 191, supposes that Walker may have introduced Shelley to Newton's spectrum-gamut parallel and so influenced a passage in *Prometheus Unbound* (IV, 256–261); this is the only connection I have ever seen made between Shelley's synesthesia and Walker.

[65] *JW,* VIII, 135; IX, 34, 36.

[66] The most extensive claims for Darwin's influence on the young (as well as the mature) Shelley appear in Carl H. Grabo, *A Newton among Poets: Shelley's Use of Science in Prometheus Unbound,* Chapel Hill, 1930, pp. 30ff.; but see also White, *Shelley,* I, 147; Carlos Baker, *Shelley's Major Poetry: The Fabric of a Vision.*

Princeton, 1948, pp. 22–25; Cameron, *The Young Shelley*, pp. 80, 240, 245, 247–248, 393–394, 397, 400; King-Hele, *Shelley*, pp. 162–164. For dating the composition of *Queen Mab*, see Cameron, pp. 239–240.

[67] *The Retrospect: Cwm Elan, 1812*, lines 69, 85; *Iliad*, III, 212.

[68] *Eyes: A Fragment* (*PW*, p. 842).

[69] See, e.g., *The Revolt of Islam*, V, xxiii, 3–5; V, xliv, 2–3 (but this is somewhat puzzling); V, st. 3, line 15 of Laone's hymn, following Spenserian st. li; IX, xxxiv, 2–3; XI, xix, 4–6; XI, xxiii, 1–2; XII, xv, 5–6.

[70] See Mrs. Shelley's notes on *The Cenci* (*PW*, pp. 334–337) and *The Witch of Atlas* (*PW*, pp. 388–389).

[71] W. B. Yeats, "The Philosophy of Shelley's Poetry" (*Essays and Introductions*, London, 1961, pp. 65–95), pp. 88–95.

[72] Edward B. Hungerford, *Shores of Darkness*, New York, 1941, pp. 216–239; Baker, *Shelley's Major Poetry*, pp. 239–254.

[73] Earl R. Wasserman, *The Subtler Language: Critical Readings of Neoclassic and Romantic Poems*, Baltimore, 1959, pp. 305–361; Wilson, *Shelley's Later Poetry*, pp. 236–255, follows Wasserman's lead.

[74] For a sampling of Shelley's comments on *Adonais*, expressed in letters ranging from June 1821 to June 1822, see *JW*, X, 270, 272, 275, 324, 328, 335, 342, 344, 351, 401; and W. S. Scott, ed., *New Shelley Letters*, London, 1948, p. 133.

[75] George E. Woodberry, ed., *The Complete Poetical Works of Shelley*, Boston, 1901, p. 624.

Chapter 2

[1] See Frederick L. Jones, "The Vision Theme in Shelley's *Alastor* and Related Works," *SP*, 44 (1947), 108–125; Baker, *Shelley's Major Poetry*, pp. 6, 9–10, 52–55, and passim. Having in mind the special usefulness of Shelley's own coinage in the title *Epipsychidion*, Baker would perhaps prefer his "psyche-epipsyche strategy" (p. 55) to "vision theme."

[2] Pliny's "De deo" (*Natural History*, Bk. II, Ch. v) is quoted near the end of Shelley's long note to *Queen Mab*, VII, 13, "There

is no God" (*PW*, p. 818). For divine sensibility, the following sentence is most relevant: "Whoever God is—provided there is a God—and in whatever region he is, he consists wholly of sense, sight and hearing, wholly of soul, wholly of mind, wholly of himself." (Loeb Classical Library trans., by H. Rackham, Cambridge, Mass., 1938, I, 179.)

[3] The best notice of the importance of Aeolian music in Shelley appears in E. von Erhardt-Siebold, "Some Inventions of the Pre-Romantic Period and Their Influence upon Literature" (*Englische Studien*, 66 [1931–1932], 347–363), pp. 361–362.

[4] Canto I, lines 352 ff. Cf. Erhardt-Siebold, "Some Inventions," p. 358.

[5] White, *Shelley*, I, 703 (brackets added). The fragment has been edited again by Lorraine Robertson, "Unpublished Verses by Shelley," *MLR*, 48 (1953), 181–184.

[6] Rogers, *Shelley at Work*, p. 263, speaks of "Mary Shelley's odd ascription" of this poem to 1818; he calls it "a Keats allegory" and associates it with the composition of *Adonais*.

[7] William Jones, 1726–1800, is quoted from *The Remains of Robert Bloomfield*, 2 vols., London, 1824, I, 108. His comments on the Aeolian harp first appeared in *Physiological Disquisitions*, London, 1781, and were excerpted in Bloomfield's *Nature's Music*, London, 1808, which is mainly a collection of literary references to the wind harp.

[8] Bloomfield, *Remains*, I, 109.

[9] Bloomfield, *Remains*, I, 114–115.

[10] *Newton Demands the Muse*, pp. 86–87.

[11] See Geoffrey Grigson, *The Harp of Aeolus and Other Essays on Art, Literature and Nature*, London, 1948, pp. 41–42.

[12] The idea of a Memnonian converse occurred to Coleridge in discussing a passage of *Paradise Lost* (IX, 1101–1110): "But the poet must likewise understand and command what Bacon calls the *vestigia communia* of the senses, the latency of all in each, and more especially as by a magical *penna duplex*, the excitement of vision by sound and the exponents of sound. Thus 'THE ECHOING WALKS BETWEEN,' [*P.L.*, IX, 1107] may be almost said to reverse the fable in tradition of the head of Memnon, in the Egyptian statue" (*Biographia Literaria*, ed. J. Shawcross, 2 vols., London, 1907, II, 103).

[13] *Par.*, XII, 1–15. The matter of Dante's influence on Shelley before 1818 is very obscure. An important discussion of some aspects of it appears in Thomas H. Vance's dissertation, "Dante and Shelley," Yale University, 1935, pp. 50–59. In my opinion the most significant item in all this is the publication in 1814 of Henry F. Cary's translation of *Purgatorio* and *Paradiso* (his version of *Inferno* had appeared in 1805–1806), though the date of Shelley's first acquaintance with Cary is unknown.

[14] *PW*, p. 14.

[15] Cf. Harold L. Hoffman, *An Odyssey of the Soul: Shelley's Alastor*, New York, 1933, p. 30: "We should recall, first, that in 'Alastor' the soul of the poet has been formed, in large part, by intercourse with natural objects. When the maiden sings to him to the accompaniment of her harp, his own soul is singing to itself. But the song is not properly his; it is the gift of something that uses the beauty of the external world as the means of addressing his soul. The idea of the soul as a harp or lyre played upon in this way is expressed several times in the poem so that its inclusion in Shelley's conception of the veiled maiden can hardly be accidental."

[16] For interesting recent discussions, see Peter Butter, *Shelley's Idols of the Cave*, Edinburgh, 1954, pp. 46–55; William H. Hildebrand, *A Study of Alastor* (Kent State University Bulletin), Kent, Ohio, 1954, pp. 46–59.

[17] Baker, pp. 58–60, argues convincingly against a common identification of the Spirit with the veiled maiden, but does not associate it, at least not directly, with the Great Parent of the invocation.

[18] Referring to this passage A. M. D. Hughes, " 'Alastor, or the Spirit of Solitude' " (*MLR*, 43 [1948], 465–470), p. 465, comments that "an invisible Spirit . . . talks . . . in a language woven of sights and sounds."

[19] *PW*, p. 14.

Chapter 3

[1] Yeats, *Essays and Introductions*, pp. 88–89.

[2] Milton, *Arcades*, line 73.

[3] V, i, 60–61.

[4] A. C. Bradley, "Notes on Shelley's *Triumph of Life*" (*MLR*, 9 [1914], 441–456), p. 445; C. D. Locock, ed., *The Poems of Percy Bysshe Shelley*, 2 vols., London, 1911, II, 484; Ellsworth Barnard, ed., *Shelley: Selected Poems, Essays, and Letters*, New York, 1944, p. 509n.

[5] *PW*, p. 428, lines 101–108.

[6] For Shelley's own translation of the *Symposium* or *Banquet*, done in 1818, see *JW*, VII, 165–220; it has been specially edited by James A. Notopoulos, *The Platonism of Shelley: A Study of Platonism and the Poetic Mind*, Durham, N. C., 1949, pp. 414–461.

[7] For comment on Shelley's special interest in Agathon, see Rogers, *Shelley at Work*, pp. 51–63.

[8] Letter, July 25, 1818, *JW*, IX, 314.

[9] Letter, Sept. 24, 1817, *JW*, IX, 246.

[10] Letter to "a Publisher," Oct. 13, 1817, *JW*, IX, 251.

[11] idem, *JW*, IX, 250–251.

[12] Baker, *Shelley's Major Poetry*, p. 82.

[13] For another, slightly different version of Shelley's, see Notopoulos, p. 509.

[14] Cf. *Par. Lost*, III, 266–267.

[15] The similar relations between Laon and Cythna on the one hand and the Serpent and the woman of the introduction on the other, along with relationships between the two pairs, are treated in Wilfred S. Dowden, "Shelley's Use of Metempsychosis in *The Revolt of Islam*," *The Rice Institute Pamphlet*, 38 (1951), 55–72. Dowden sees the Serpent and the woman of the introduction as reincarnations of Laon and Cythna; he does not seem to understand that the Serpent and the Morning Star are one (i.e., Lucifer) and generally fails to see the importance for all this of Shelley's Venus symbolism.

[16] For scientific aspects of this and other passages of Shelley which refer to volcanic action, see G. M. Matthews, "A Volcano's Voice in Shelley," *ELH*, 24 (1957), 191–228.

[17] Stewart C. Wilcox, "The Sources, Symbolism, and Unity of Shelley's Skylark," *SP*, 46 (1949), 560–576.

[18] *For Lancelot Andrewes: Essays on Style and Order*, Garden City, N. Y., 1929, pp. 135–136.

[19] Eliot, p. 135.

[20] Eliot, p. 136.

[21] A. E. Housman, letter, *TLS*, Dec. 20, 1928, p. 1011; A. Eiloart, "Shelley's 'Skylark': The 'Silver Sphere' " (*Notes and Queries*, 161 [1931], 4–8), pp. 7–8. For a recent interesting discussion of this identification, see King-Hele, *Shelley*, pp. 228–229.

[22] But see Chapter 2, n. 6, above.

[23] *The Works of John Milton*, gen. ed., F. A. Patterson, 18 vols., New York, 1931–1938, XII, 153, 155.

[24] See, e.g., Carl Grabo, *The Magic Plant: The Growth of Shelley's Thought*, Chapel Hill, 1936, p. 409; Ellsworth Barnard, ed., *Shelley: Selected Poems, Essays, and Letters*, p. 504n; Kenneth N. Cameron, ed., *Percy Bysshe Shelley: Selected Poetry and Prose*, New York, 1951, p. 522. All such favorable views of the "Shape all light" have recently been challenged by Bloom, *Shelley's Mythmaking*, pp. 267ff.

[25] Baker, *Shelley's Major Poetry*, p. 266; Grabo, *The Magic Plant*, p. 409; Yeats, *Essays and Introductions*, pp. 88, 89, 94. Concerning the last, cf. Bloom, *Shelley's Mythmaking*, p. 270: "Yeats had nothing to say of the Shape," etc.

[26] Baker, p. 260.

[27] A. C. Bradley, "Notes on Shelley's *Triumph of Life*," p. 441.

[28] See, e.g., John Todhunter, "Notes on 'The Triumph of Life' " (*The Shelley Society's Publications*, First Series, No. 1, Part I [1888], 73–80), p. 78; Grabo, *The Magic Plant*, p. 406; Barnard, ed., *Shelley: Selected Poems, Essays, and Letters*, p. 494n.

[29] Butter, *Shelley's Idols of the Cave*, p. 30; yet Butter, who had read Yeats on *The Triumph of Life*, insisted (pp. 30, 145) on equating the "Shape all light" with the sun, not Venus. In an article, which I did not see until this book was completed, "Sun and Shape in Shelley's *The Triumph of Life*," *RES*, New Series, 13 (1962), 40–51, Butter writes generally as though the poem opposed higher and lower Venuses, but partly withdraws the identification of Life with a lower Venus (p. 43), and explicitly rejects Yeats's view of the "Shape all light" (p. 41n).

[30] Baker, p. 259.

[31] This and all subsequent translations from the *Commedia* are quoted from John D. Sinclair's versions of *Inferno*, *Purgatorio*, and *Paradiso*, as reprinted by the Oxford University Press, 3 vols., New York, 1959–1961.

[32] See Bradley, "Notes on Shelley's *Triumph of Life*," p. 449.

[33] *PW*, p. 517n.

Chapter 4

[1] Letter to Gisborne, June 18, 1822, *JW*, X, 401.

[2] "Fragments Connected with *Epipsychidion*," lines 38–39 (*PW*, p. 426).

[3] Mary recorded Shelley's reading of *Corinne* in December, 1818; she herself read, or read in, the novel at least three times: early in 1815, in December, 1818, and in November, 1820. See Frederick L. Jones, ed., *Mary Shelley's Journal*, Norman, Okla., 1947, pp. 39, 113, 140–141. For Emilia's reading the borrowed copy, see White, *Shelley*, II, 249.

[4] *Corinne ou l' Italie*, ed. Mme. Necker de Saussure, Paris, n.d., p. 32; my trans.

[5] John Laird, *Our Minds and their Bodies*, London, 1925, p. 119.

[6] But of the thirteen-line conclusion, or *envoi*, nine lines rhyme irregularly.

[7] For Shelley's translation of this canzone, the first in Dante's *Convivio*, see *PW*, pp. 726–727.

[8] *Shelley*, II, 608.

[9] G. Wilson Knight, *The Starlit Dome: Studies in the Poetry of Vision*, rev. edn., New York, 1960, p. 235.

[10] Cf. White, *Shelley*, II, 268–269.

[11] Joseph Barrell, *Shelley and the Thought of His Time: A Study in the History of Ideas*, New Haven, 1947, p. 169.

[12] Barrell, p. 169.

[13] Barrell, p. 169.

[14] *PW*, p. 411; my trans. Shelley drew the motto from Emilia's essay *Il vero amore*; see White, *Shelley*, II, 257.

Chapter 5

[1] Hungerford, *Shores of Darkness*, pp. 216–239; Baker, *Shelley's Major Poetry*, pp. 239–254.

[2] Wasserman, *The Subtler Language*, pp. 305–361; this essay first appeared as "*Adonais:* Progressive Revelation as a Poetic Mode," *ELH*, 21 (1954), 274–326.

[3] Hungerford, pp. 219–220, 222, 235–237.

[4] Hungerford, p. 236.

[5] Hungerford, pp. 238–239.

[6] This conjecture involves assumptions about Spenserian adaptations of the Venus-Adonis myth in *Astrophel;* in the so-called "Lay of Clorinda" (ostensibly by the Countess of Pembroke but possibly by Spenser himself); and in the "Garden-of-Adonis" canto of *The Faerie Queene* (Book III, Canto VI). Without attempting to develop this here, I will simply state my belief that Shelley may have read *Astrophel* and the "Lay of Clorinda" as one poem—a poem covertly sustaining and transforming in the latter part the myth which is adapted in the former. Read so, this "poem" has striking structural and other similarities to *Adonais*. For supporting and suggestive evidence for all this, see two articles by T. P. Harrison, Jr.: "Spenser and the Earlier Pastoral Elegy," and "Spenser and Shelley's *Adonais*," *The University of Texas Studies in English*, 13 (1933), 36–53 and 54–63. Consult also S. C. Wilcox, "Shelley's *Adonais* XX, 172–177," *The Explicator*, 9 (No. 6, 1951), item 39.

[7] Baker, pp. 246–247.

[8] Baker, pp. 247–249.

[9] *PW*, p. 720.

[10] Wasserman, p. 324n.

[11] Wasserman, p. 350.

[12] Wasserman, pp. 350–351.

[13] Wasserman, pp. 351–352.

[14] Wasserman, p. 352.

[15] Wasserman, p. 352.

[16] Wasserman, pp. 350–351.

[17] Wilson, *Shelley's Later Poetry*, p. 237.

[18] Wasserman, pp. 324–325.

[19] Wasserman, pp. 342–343.

[20] Throughout this chapter I have departed from practice in *PW* by numbering stanzas in Arabic rather than Roman.

[21] Wasserman, p. 353.

[22] Wasserman, p. 353.

[23] Wasserman, p. 352.

[24] *Adonais,* 4, 3.

[25] Wasserman, p. 333.

[26] *JW,* VII, 124. My interpretation appears to gain support from the discovery of Rogers, *Shelley at Work,* pp. 264–265, that in a draft of *Adonais,* stanza 4, Shelley actually substituted the name "Urania" for the words "great poetry."

[27] *JW,* VII, 115.

[28] *JW,* VII, 131.

[29] *JW,* VII, 131.

[30] Vance's dissertation, "Dante and Shelley," pp. 83–88, cites *Par.,* I, 1–3; I, 109–117; XXIII, 46–48; XXVII, 4–5; XXIX, 136–145; XXXIII, 30–32.

[31] The line renders parts of *Par.,* XXIX, 136–138; Cary's synesthetic figure has no equivalent in the original.

[32] Andrew Lang, trans., *Theocritus, Bion, and Moschus,* London, 1901, p. 202.

[33] *JW,* VII, 137.

[34] *Fragments of an Unfinished Drama,* lines 173–174 (*PW,* p. 486).

Chapter 6

[1] Richard Garnett, ed., *Relics of Shelley,* London, 1862, pp. 20–25. In this edn. *Orpheus* is 110 lines long; it appeared revised and expanded to 124 lines in William Michael Rossetti, ed., *The Poetical Works of Percy Bysshe Shelley,* 2 vols., London, 1870, II, 333–336.

[2] *Relics,* p. 20.

[3] Locock, ed., *The Poems of Percy Bysshe Shelley,* II, 516–517.

[4] See Rogers, *Shelley at Work,* pp. 238–246, and A. Koszul, "Inédits italiens de Shelley," *Rev. de Litt. Comp.,* 2 (1922), 471–477.

[5] See Locock's edn., II, 517, for the following revelation of his editorial and critical instincts: "[Mary's] application of the same metaphor to Sgricci, in her diary for Dec. 20, 1820, makes it . . . probable that the eloquence complained of was not Shelley's but Sgricci's."

[6] White, *Shelley*, II, 189 and 590–591; Butter, *Shelley's Idols of the Cave*, p. 101.

[7] But for a respectful opinion and a conviction that only Shelley could have been the author, see H. B. Forman, "The Improvvisatore Sgricci in Relation to Shelley," *Gentleman's Magazine*, January 1880, pp. 115–123, esp. p. 121.

[8] *Relics*, p. 20.

[9] See Mary Shelley's note, *PW*, p. 271. For details of composition, see Lawrence J. Zillman, ed., *Shelley's* Prometheus Unbound: *A Variorum Edition*, Seattle, 1959, pp. 3–6.

[10] For copious illustration, see Zillman's *Variorum*, "Critical Notes," pp. 302–630. An extremely valuable recent discussion of the poem is in Wilson, *Shelley's Later Poetry*, pp. 40–101, 256–279.

[11] *An Hymne of Heavenly Love*, line 83.

[12] Notopoulos, *The Platonism of Shelley*, pp. 256–257.

[13] Shelley's own trans., *JW*, VII, 190.

[14] Synesthetic discussion of these lines is markedly puzzling. June Downey, "Literary Synesthesia," p. 496, synesthetically equated "Aeolian music" and "sea-green." Fogle, *The Imagery of Keats and Shelley*, p. 129, considering this a "rather ambiguous example" of Miss Downey's "tonal vision," stated: "Both *Aeolian music* and *sea-green plumes winnow* the dawn; there is no reason to suppose that the music is sea-green." Bloom, *Shelley's Mythmaking*, pp. 116–117, wrote: "Fogle has what appears to me to be a definitive discussion of synaesthetic imagery in Shelley, in which he analyzes the final [i.e., the last three] lines of this passage." So Bloom's unique comment on synesthesia concerns a passage which the definitive authority says is not synesthetic.

[15] For a suggestion that lines 98–110 have an allegorical precedent in Plato's *Statesman* see E. M. W. Tillyard, letter, *TLS*, Sept. 29, 1932, p. 691. Consult also Irene H. Chayes, "Plato's *Statesman* Myth in Shelley and Blake," *Comp. Lit.*, 13 (1961), 358–369.

[16] A specially notable complexity, which I have not tried to cope with, may involve relations between the stream-of-sound and lore concerning volcanic action; see Matthews, "A Volcano's Voice in Shelley," pp. 204–224.

[17] This shell has frequently been compared with a famous one in Wordsworth, *The Excursion*, IV, 1135–1144; see Zillman's *Variorum*, pp. 534–535, and Bloom, pp. 135–136. A much better

comparison, in my opinion, is with a "magic shell" celebrated in Thomas Moore's poem, "The Genius of Harmony," which first appeared in *Epistles, Odes, and Other Poems,* London, 1806. Shelley read Moore's book in 1817 (see Jones, ed., *Mary Shelley's Journal,* p. 90), and the shell of "The Genius of Harmony" may have influenced *The Revolt of Islam,* VII, xiii, 1–7. The conclusion of Moore's poem is synesthetically curious, being intended, according to one of the author's many erudite notes, "to represent the analogy between the notes of music and the prismatic colors" by referring to a seven-gemmed diadem's "soft iris of harmonious light" (p. 54). Moore adds: "Cassiodorus, whose idea I may be supposed to have borrowed, says, in a letter upon music to Boetius, '*Ut diadema oculis, varia luce gemmarum, sic cythara diversitate soni, blanditur auditui.*' "

[18] *The Starlit Dome,* p. 212.

[19] PW, pp. 277–278.

[20] *A Newton among Poets,* pp. 140ff. See also King-Hele, *Shelley: His Thought and Work,* pp. 188–195.

[21] See, e.g., White, *Shelley,* II, 129.

[22] See Isaacs, *The Background of Modern Poetry,* pp. 31–33; Fogle, *The Imagery of Keats and Shelley,* pp. 49–54; Knight, *The Starlit Dome,* p. 221.

[23] *Par. Lost,* VI, 748ff. A valuable recent article dealing with Shelley's passage in relationship to Milton is Ants Oras, "The Multitudinous Orb: Some Miltonic Elements in Shelley," *MLQ,* 16 (1955), 247–257.

Chapter 7

[1] *PW,* p. 158.

WORKS CITED

Babbitt, Irving. *The New Laokoon: An Essay on the Confusion of the Arts.* Boston and New York, 1910.

Baker, Carlos. *Shelley's Major Poetry: The Fabric of a Vision.* Princeton, 1948.

Barrell, Joseph. *Shelley and the Thought of His Time: A Study in the History of Ideas.* New Haven, 1947.

Bloom, Harold. *Shelley's Mythmaking.* New Haven, 1959.

Bloomfield, Robert. *The Remains of Robert Bloomfield.* 2 vols. London, 1824.

Bradley, A. C. "Notes on Shelley's *Triumph of Life*," *MLR*, 9 (1914), 441–456.

Butter, Peter. *Shelley's Idols of the Cave.* Edinburgh, 1954.

———. "Sun and Shape in Shelley's *The Triumph of Life*," *RES*, New Series, 13 (1962), 40–51.

Cameron, Kenneth N. *The Young Shelley: Genesis of a Radical.* New York, 1950.

Chayes, Irene H. "Plato's *Statesman* Myth in Shelley and Blake," *Comp. Lit.*, 13 (1961), 358–369.

Coleridge, S. T. *Biographia Literaria,* ed. J. Shawcross. 2 vols. London, 1907.

Dante. *The Divine Comedy,* trans. John D. Sinclair. 3 vols. New York, 1959–1961.

Darwin, Erasmus. *The Botanic Garden,* 4th edn. 2 vols. London, 1799.

———. *The Temple of Nature.* London, 1803.

Dowden, Wilfred S. "Shelley's Use of Metempsychosis in *The Revolt of Islam*," *The Rice Institute Pamphlet*, 38 (1951), 55–72.

Downey, June E. "Literary Synesthesia," *Journal of Philosophy, Psychology, and Scientific Methods*, 9 (1912), 490–498.

———. *Creative Imagination: Studies in the Psychology of Literature*. New York, 1929.

Eiloart, A. "Shelley's 'Skylark': The 'Silver Sphere,'" *Notes and Queries*, 161 (1931), 4–8.

Eliot, T. S. *For Lancelot Andrewes: Essays on Style and Order*. Garden City, N. Y., 1929.

Empson, William. *Seven Types of Ambiguity*, 2nd edn. London, 1947.

Engstrom, Alfred G. "In Defence of Synaesthesia in Literature," *PQ*, 25 (1946), 1–19.

Erhardt-Siebold, Erika von. "Synästhesien in der englischen Dichtung des 19. Jahrhunderts: Ein ästhetisch-psychologischer Versuch," *Englische Studien*, 53 (1919–1920), 1–157; 196–334.

———. "Some Inventions of the Pre-Romantic Period and Their Influence upon Literature," *Englische Studien*, 66 (1931–1932), 347–363.

———. "Harmony of the Senses in English, German, and French Romanticism," *PMLA*, 47 (1932), 577–592.

Firkins, Oscar W. *Power and Elusiveness in Shelley*. Minneapolis, 1937.

Fogle, Richard H. *The Imagery of Keats and Shelley: A Comparative Study*. Chapel Hill, 1949.

Forman, H. B. "The Improvvisatore Sgricci in Relation to Shelley," *Gentleman's Magazine*, January, 1880, pp. 115–123.

Grabo, Carl H. *A Newton among Poets: Shelley's Use of Science in Prometheus Unbound*. Chapel Hill, 1930.

———. *The Magic Plant: The Growth of Shelley's Thought*. Chapel Hill, 1936.

Grigson, Geoffrey. *The Harp of Aeolus and Other Essays on Art, Literature and Nature*. London, 1948.

Harrison, T. P., Jr. "Spenser and the Earlier Pastoral Elegy," *The University of Texas Studies in English*, 13 (1933), 36–53.

———. "Spenser and Shelley's *Adonais*," *The University of Texas Studies in English*, 13 (1933), 54–63.

Hildebrand, William H. A *Study of Alastor*. (Kent State University Bulletin.) Kent, Ohio, 1954.

Hoffman, Harold L. *An Odyssey of the Soul: Shelley's Alastor*. New York, 1933.

Housman, A. E. Letter, *TLS*, Dec. 20, 1928, p. 1011.

Hughes, A. M. D. " 'Alastor, or the Spirit of Solitude,' " *MLR*, 43 (1948), 465–470.

Hungerford, Edward B. *Shores of Darkness*. New York, 1941.

Isaacs, J. *The Background of Modern Poetry*. New York, 1958.

Jones, Frederick L. "The Vision Theme in Shelley's *Alastor* and Related Works," *SP*, 44 (1947), 108–125.

———, ed. *Mary Shelley's Journal*. Norman, Okla., 1947.

King-Hele, Desmond. *Shelley: His Thought and Work*. London, 1960.

Knight, G. Wilson. *The Starlit Dome: Studies in the Poetry of Vision*, rev. edn. New York, 1960.

Koszul, A. "Inédits italiens de Shelley," *Rev. de Litt. Comp.*, 2 (1922), 471–477.

Laird, John. *Our Minds and their Bodies*. London, 1925.

Lang, Andrew, trans. *Theocritus, Bion, and Moschus*. London, 1901.

Locke, John. *An Essay concerning Human Understanding*, ed. Alexander C. Fraser. 2 vols. Oxford, 1894.

MacLean, Kenneth. *John Locke and English Literature of the Eighteenth Century*. New Haven, 1936.

Matthews, G. M. "A Volcano's Voice in Shelley," *ELH*, 24 (1957), 191–228.

Milton, John. *The Works of John Milton*, gen. ed. F. A. Patterson. 18 vols. New York, 1931–1938.

Moore, Thomas. *Epistles, Odes, and Other Poems*. London, 1806.

Newton, Isaac. *Opticks*, ed. E. T. Whittaker. New York, 1931.

Nicolson, Marjorie H. *Newton Demands the Muse*. Princeton, 1946.

Notopoulos, James A. *The Platonism of Shelley: A Study of Platonism and the Poetic Mind*. Durham, N. C., 1949.

Oras, Ants. "The Multitudinous Orb: Some Miltonic Elements in Shelley," *MLQ*, 16 (1955), 247–257.

Pliny. *Natural History*, trans. H. Rackham. Vol. I. Cambridge, Mass., 1938.

Robertson, Lorraine. "Unpublished Verses by Shelley," *MLR*, 48 (1953), 181–184.

Rogers, Neville. *Shelley at Work: A Critical Inquiry*. Oxford, 1956.

Schier, Donald S. *Louis Bertrand Castel, Anti-Newtonian Scientist*. Cedar Rapids, Iowa, 1941.

Shaftesbury, Anthony, Earl of. *Second Characters, or The Language of Forms*, ed. Benjamin Rand. Cambridge, Eng., 1914.

Shelley, P. B. *Relics of Shelley*, ed. Richard Garnett. London, 1862.

———. *The Poetical Works of Percy Bysshe Shelley*, ed. William Michael Rossetti. 2 vols. London, 1870.

———. *The Complete Poetical Works of Shelley*, ed. George E. Woodberry. Boston, 1901.

———. *The Complete Poetical Works of Percy Bysshe Shelley*, ed. Thomas Hutchinson. London, 1934. (First published, Oxford, 1904.)

———. *The Poems of Percy Bysshe Shelley*, ed. C. D. Locock. 2 vols. London, 1911.

———. *The Complete Works of Percy Bysshe Shelley*, eds. Roger Ingpen and Walter E. Peck. 10 vols. London and New York, 1926–1930.

———. *Shelley: Selected Poems, Essays, and Letters*, ed. Ellsworth Barnard. New York, 1944.

———. *Percy Bysshe Shelley: Selected Poetry and Prose*, ed. Kenneth N. Cameron. New York, 1951.

———. *Shelley's* Prometheus Unbound: *A Variorum Edition*, ed. Lawrence J. Zillman. Seattle, 1959.

———. *New Shelley Letters*, ed. W. S. Scott. London, 1948.

Shine, Hill and Helen C. *The Quarterly Review under Gifford: Identification of Contributors, 1809–1824*. Chapel Hill, 1949.

Staël, Madame de. *Corinne ou l' Italie*, ed. Mme. Necker de Saussure. Paris, n.d.

———. *De l' Allemagne*, ed. Jean de Pange. 5 vols. Paris, 1958–1960.

Stanford, William B. *Greek Metaphor: Studies in Theory and Practice*. Oxford, 1936.

Suddard, S. J. Mary. *Keats, Shelley and Shakespeare: Studies and Essays in English Literature*. Cambridge, Eng., 1912.

Tillyard, E. M. W. Letter, *TLS*, Sept. 29, 1932, p. 691.

Todhunter, John. "Notes on 'The Triumph of Life,'" *The Shelley*

Society's Publications, First Series, No. 1, Part I (1888), 73–80.

Ullmann, Stephen. *The Principles of Semantics*. Glasgow, 1951.

Vance, Thomas H. "Dante and Shelley." Yale University dissertation, 1935.

Voltaire. *Oeuvres Complètes de Voltaire*. 52 vols. Paris, 1877–1885.

Walker, Adam. *A System of Familiar Philosophy: In Twelve Lectures*. 2 vols. London, 1802.

Wasserman, Earl R. *The Subtler Language: Critical Readings of Neoclassic and Romantic Poems*. Baltimore, 1959.

Wellek, Albert. "Das Doppelempfinden im abendländischen Altertum und Mittelalter," *Archiv für die gesamte Psychologie*, 80 (1931), 120–166.

———. "Renaissance- und Barock-Synästhesie: Die Geschichte des Doppelempfindens im 16. und 17. Jahrhundert," *Deutsche Vierteljahrsschrift für Literaturwissenschaft und Geistesgeschichte*, 9 (1931), 534–584.

———. "Zur Geschichte und Kritik der Synästhesie-Forschung," *Archiv für die gesamte Psychologie*, 79 (1931), 325–384.

———. "Das Doppelempfinden im 18. Jahrhundert," *Deutsche Vierteljahrsschrift für Literaturwissenschaft und Geistesgeschichte*, 14 (1936), 75–102.

White, Newman I. *Shelley*. 2 vols. New York, 1940.

———, ed. *The Unextinguished Hearth: Shelley and His Contemporary Critics*. Durham, N. C., 1938.

Wilcox, Stewart C. "The Sources, Symbolism, and Unity of Shelley's *Skylark*," *SP*, 46 (1949), 560–576.

———. "Shelley's *Adonais* XX, 172–177," *The Explicator*, 9 (No. 6, 1951), item 39.

Wilson, Milton. *Shelley's Later Poetry: A Study of His Prophetic Imagination*. New York, 1959.

Yeats, W. B. *Essays and Introductions*. London, 1961.

INDEX*

* Works referred to, except Shelley's, appear under author's name.

Index